HOUGHTON MIFFLIN SOCIAL STUDIES

Some People I Know

*S*ome people I know like to chatter,
  while others speak hardly a word;
  some think there is nothing the matter
  with being completely absurd;
  some are impossibly serious,
  while others are absolute fun;
  some are reserved and mysterious,
  while others shine bright as the sun.

Jack Prelutsky

Beverly J. Armento
Gary B. Nash
Christopher L. Salter
Karen K. Wixson

Some People I Know

Houghton Mifflin Company • Boston

Atlanta • Dallas • Geneva, Illinois • Princeton, New Jersey • Palo Alto • Toronto

Consultants

Program Consultants

Edith M. Guyton
Associate Professor of Early
  Childhood Education
Georgia State University
Atlanta, Georgia

Gail Hobbs
Associate Professor of Geography
Pierce College
Woodland Hills, California

Charles Peters
Reading Consultant
Oakland Schools
Pontiac, Michigan

Cathy Riggs-Salter
Social Studies Consultant
Hartsburg, Missouri

Alfredo Schifini
Limited English Proficiency Consultant
Los Angeles, California

George Paul Schneider
Associate Director
  of General Programs
Department of Museum Education
Art Institute of Chicago
Chicago, Illinois

Twyla Stewart
Center for Academic Interinstitutional
  Programs
University of California—Los Angeles
Los Angeles, California

Scott Waugh
Associate Professor of History
University of California—Los Angeles
Los Angeles, California

Teacher Reviewers

David E. Beer (Grade 5)
Weisser Park Elementary
Fort Wayne, Indiana

Jan Coleman (Grades 6–7)
Thornton Junior High
Fremont, California

Shawn Edwards
  (Grades 1–3)
Jackson Park Elementary
University City, Missouri

Barbara J. Fech (Grade 6)
Martha Ruggles School
Chicago, Illinois

Deborah M. Finkel
  (Grade 4)
Los Angeles Unified
  School District,
  Region G
South Pasadena,
  California

Jim Fletcher (Grades 5, 8)
La Loma Junior High
Modesto, California

Susan M. Gilliam
  (Grade 1)
Roscoe Elementary
Los Angeles, California

Vicki Stroud Gonterman
  (Grade 2)
Gibbs International
  Studies Magnet School
Little Rock, Arkansas

Lorraine Hood (Grade 2)
Fresno Unified School
  District
Fresno, California

Jean Jamgochian
  (Grade 5)
Haycock Gifted and
  Talented Center
Fairfax County, Virginia

Susan Kirk-Davalt
  (Grade 5)
Crowfoot Elementary
Lebanon, Oregon

Mary Molyneaux-Leahy
  (Grade 3)
Bridgeport Elementary
Bridgeport, Pennsylvania

Sharon Oviatt
  (Grades 1–3)
Keysor Elementary
Kirkwood, Missouri

Jayne B. Perala (Grade 1)
Cave Spring Elementary
Roanoke, Virginia

Carol Siefkin (K)
Garfield Elementary
Sacramento, California

Norman N. Tanaka
  (Grade 3)
Martin Luther King Jr.
  Elementary
Sacramento, California

John Tyler (Grades 5, 8)
Groton School
Groton, Massachusetts

Portia W. Vaughn
  (Grades 1–3)
School District 11
Colorado Springs,
  Colorado

ISBN: 0-395-52725-2
  GHIJ-VH-998765432

Development by Ligature, Inc.

Acknowledgments

    Grateful acknowledgment is made
for the use of the material listed below.
ii From "Some People I Know" by Jack
Prelutsky from *The Random House Book*
of Poetry for Children, selected and
introduced by Jack Prelutsky. Copyright
© 1983 by Random House. Reprinted by
permission of the publisher.

–Continued on page 192.

From Your Authors

This picture shows a bunch of bananas on their way to market. We've given them faces, just to have some fun. In Unit 1 you can read more about how bananas grow and who the people are who get them to market.

In this book you will read about many other people and places. You will learn about life now and long ago. We'll talk about our special country, the United States of America. You will meet some real people and learn how they live.

Some of the stories in this book will make you laugh! Others will make you think and want to try new things. We hope you will like your new book.

Beverly J. Armento
Professor of Social Studies
Director, Center for Business and
Economic Education
Georgia State University

Christopher L. Salter
Professor and Chair
Department of Geography
University of Missouri

Gary B. Nash
Professor of History
University of California—Los Angeles

Karen K. Wixson
Associate Professor of Education
University of Michigan

Contents

Charts, Diagrams, and Timelines

These pictures give you facts about the people, places, and things you are studying.

Parts of a Banana Plant

Leaf

Stem

Banana Bunch

Stalk

Roots

Maps

Each map in this book tells a story about a place.

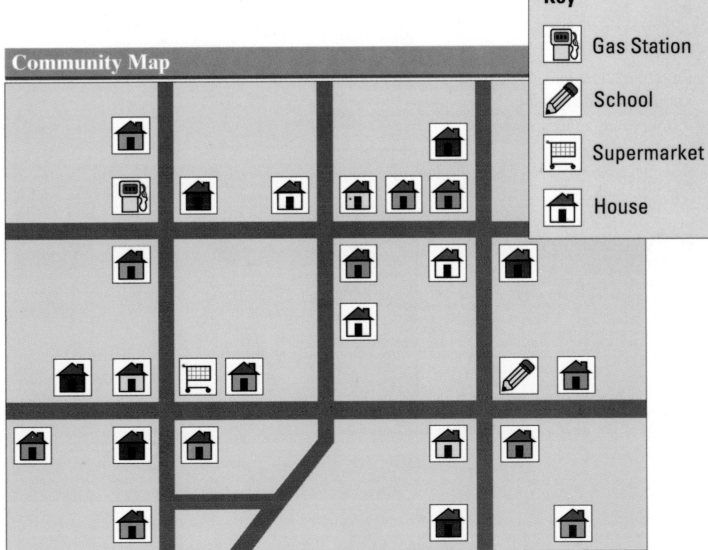

Community Map

Key

🔲 Gas Station

✏️ School

🛒 Supermarket

🏠 House

Starting Out

This is your book.
Let's get to know it.

The number tells you
which lesson it is.

The title tells you
what the lesson is about.

Read the question.
Think about the question
as you read the lesson.

This is a word you
will learn in this lesson.

LESSON 6

A Long Time Here

In beauty, I shall walk.
In beauty, you shall be my picture.
In beauty, you shall be my song.

from the Navajo Nightway Ceremony

THINK

What traditions has
Melanie learned
from her family?

Key Word

weave

This poem is about the land where Melanie
Begaye *(beh GAY)* lives. Melanie is eight years
old. She lives with her family near Round
Rock, Arizona. Her ancestors have lived on
this land for many years, since before the
United States became a country. Melanie and
her family are Navajos.

90

The land where Melanie lives is beautiful, but little rain falls there. Sometimes people have to bring water from far away. There is little grass. The land is tan and brown with big red rocks.

There are no big cities near where Melanie lives. There are no tall buildings. Melanie can look out across the land and see for a long way. She can see mountains in the distance.

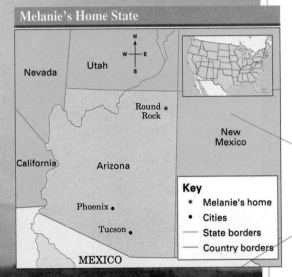

Melanie's Home State

Nevada
Utah
N
W E
S
Round Rock
New Mexico
California
Arizona
Phoenix
Tucson
MEXICO

Key
• Melanie's home
• Cities
— State borders
— Country borders

A map tells you where things are.

Photos tell you what that place is like.

Maps and photos help you understand the lesson.

91

Moving On

Pictures and words work together.
Together they help you learn.

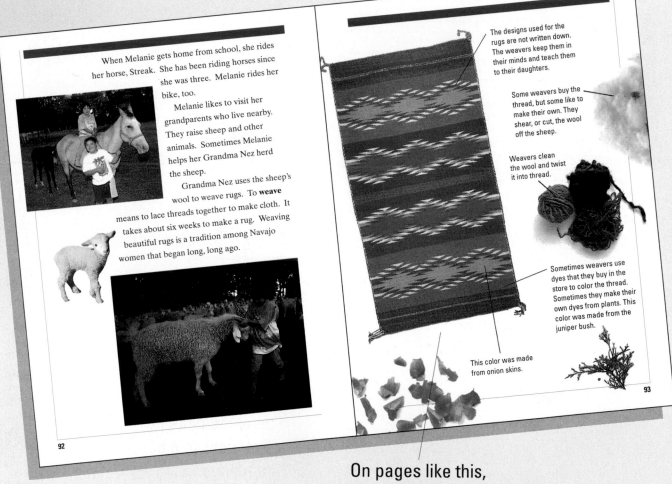

When Melanie gets home from school, she rides her horse, Streak. She has been riding horses since she was three. Melanie rides her bike, too.

Melanie likes to visit her grandparents who live nearby. They raise sheep and other animals. Sometimes Melanie helps her Grandma Nez herd the sheep.

Grandma Nez uses the sheep's wool to weave rugs. To **weave** means to lace threads together to make cloth. It takes about six weeks to make a rug. Weaving beautiful rugs is a tradition among Navajo women that began long, long ago.

92

The designs used for the rugs are not written down. The weavers keep them in their minds and teach them to their daughters.

Some weavers buy the thread, but some like to make their own. They shear, or cut, the wool off the sheep.

Weavers clean the wool and twist it into thread.

Sometimes weavers use dyes that they buy in the store to color the thread. Sometimes they make their own dyes from plants. This color was made from the juniper bush.

This color was made from onion skins.

93

On pages like this,
you will take a close look
at something in the lesson.
Here you take a close look
at weaving.

Melanie's Aunt Lucy weaves, too. In this picture, Aunt Lucy is just beginning to weave a rug.

Melanie learns other things from her family. During the winter, Melanie's grandparents like to tell stories. After supper, when the sun sets, the family sits around the fire. Melanie's grandparents tell about the smart coyote who is always playing tricks on others. Coyote stories are a tradition with the Navajo people.

Melanie has learned many family traditions. She has learned to share and to care for others. She often takes care of her little brother, Merrell. She has learned to share food and clothes with people who need them.

Melanie has also learned to understand and to speak some Navajo words. She has learned to care for sheep. Her grandparents have taught her coyote stories. Someday, she may teach all these things to her grandchildren.

REVIEW

1. What traditions has Melanie learned from her family?
2. Where do Melanie's grandma and Aunt Lucy get their rug designs?
3. The picture on pages 90–91 shows the land where Melanie lives. Draw a picture of the things around your home.

95

This part helps you review
what you have read.
The answers to the questions
are in the lesson.

This is the page number.
It is always in a corner
of the page.
It helps you keep your place.

Learning More

You can learn in many ways.
Special pages in the book
help you to learn more.

Do you like to explore?
This page tells you how.

Some pages tell you
about ideas and about
ways of doing things.
This page tells you
how to share with others.

EXPLORE

Where Food Comes From

You found out where peanut butter comes from.
Now you can find out where stores get other
foods, too.

Get Ready
1. Talk about where you think other foods
   come from.
2. Get paper, a pencil, crayons, and yarn.

Find Out
1. Look at the diagram. See where the food
   comes from.
2. Find out where other foods come
   from. Look at labels on boxes
   and cans of food. Talk to people.
   Use other books, too.

Apples from Washington

Where Does Your Food Come From?

Fish from Maine

Cheese from Wisconsin

Supermarket

18

THINK ABOUT WORKING TOGETHER

Working and Sharing

One Navajo custom Melanie learned is to share
with others. When working on a school project,
everyone should share, too.

People working as a group share things such as
scissors and glue. They also share their ideas. They
learn from each other, and they help each other.
Everyone has a chance to have an important part.

Read the list below. It tells what to do when you
work in a group.
1. Tell the others your ideas about the project.
2. Listen to the ideas of others.
3. Help to do the work.

96

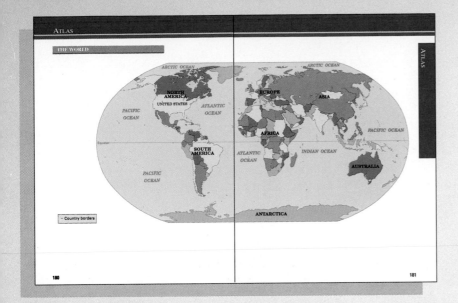

Look for more maps
in the back of the book.
This is a map of the world.

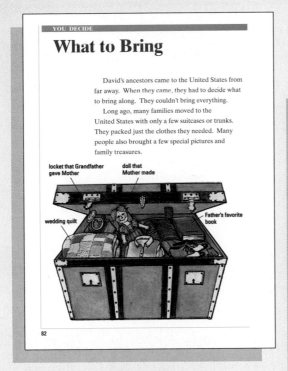

What would you do?
This page helps you decide.

Your book has stories
and poems, too.
Stories and poems
help you learn.

Unit 1

Depending on Others

People buying, people selling
Food from everywhere—
Apples, oranges, cheese, bananas,
Peanut butter, pears.

People pick and pack and ship
The food that's in our store,
And so the food is always there
When we go back for more.

The Lunch Box Story

THINK

How do you depend
on people?

Key Word

depend

"It's time for lunch! What is
in my lunch box today? Yum!
A peanut butter sandwich,
a banana, and . . . Hey! What
are all those people doing in my
lunch box? Who are they?"

Believe it or not, all of these people helped make Amy's lunch. *Someone* had to grow the peanuts for her peanut butter sandwich. *Someone* had to pick the bananas. *Someone* had to get them to the store.

Many people do special jobs to bring food to you. You depend on them. If you **depend** on people, it means that you need them. You depend on people for many things besides food. Look around you. Who made your shoes? Who made your books? What other people do you depend on to make things for you?

REVIEW

1. How do you depend on people?
2. Who helped make your lunch?
3. Draw a picture of some of the people you depend on.

Finding Places

Think of all the people you depend on to help make your lunch. Many of them work in your community. Look at the picture below. It shows a real community. People living here depend on the supermarket. They also depend on the gas station and on the school.

A map is like a picture taken from above. Artists draw the streets. They put in small pictures, or symbols, to stand for the buildings.

The map on this page shows another community. Look at the **map key** above the map. It explains the symbols on the map. What does each symbol stand for?

Find the symbol for a supermarket on the map key. Then find the same symbol on the map. It shows where the supermarket is. What symbol stands for a school? Point to the school.

Key

Gas Station

School

Supermarket

House

Community Map

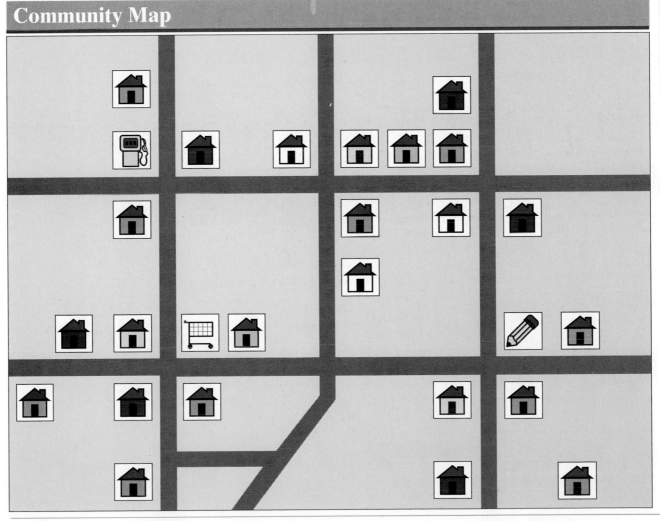

A map also shows directions. On a map, **north** is usually toward the top. **South** is usually toward the bottom. If north is at the top, then the direction to your right is **east.** The direction to your left is **west.**

How can you remember all this? Map artists add something to help. It is called a **compass rose.** It shows directions. Find the compass rose on the map. *N* for north is at the top. *S* for south is at the bottom. What letter stands for east? What letter stands for west?

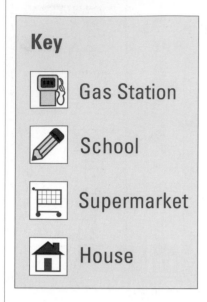

Key

Gas Station

School

Supermarket

House

Community Map

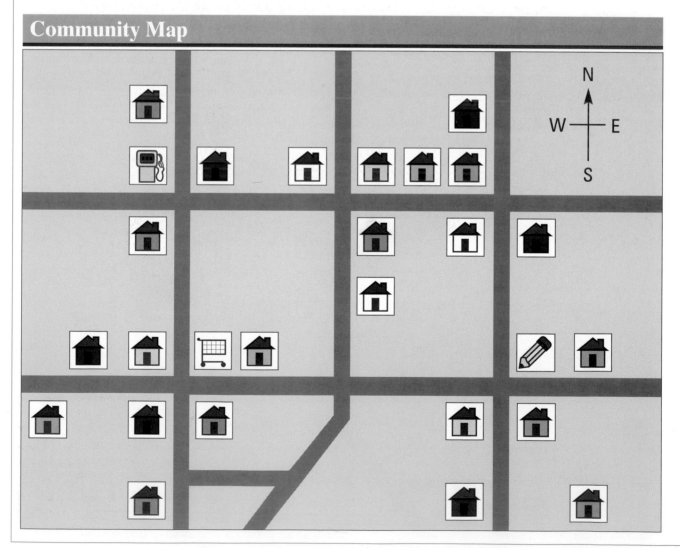

Point to the supermarket. Move your finger from there to the gas station. You moved toward the top of the map. What direction is that? The gas station is north of the supermarket.

People use maps to find their way from one place to another. Pretend you live in the green house on the map. You want to go to the supermarket. Put your finger on your house and move it one block west. Turn the corner and go one block south.

Find a different path home. Which directions did you travel?

Try It!

Find and trace a path from the green house to the school. Tell which directions you traveled.

People and Peanuts

THINK

What kinds of work do people do to make peanut butter?

Key Words

crops
harvest
factory

You depend on farmers to grow your food. Josh Wambles's dad is a farmer in Alabama. He grows one of the foods some people like best—peanuts.

Josh is in the second grade. He likes to help his dad on the farm. Josh and his family love to eat the peanuts they grow on their farm. They roast, boil, or fry them. How do you like to eat peanuts?

Josh's farm has rich, sandy soil. Peanuts need sandy soil and long, hot summers to grow. Josh's dad also grows other crops. **Crops** are the plants farmers grow to sell. The map shows the fields on Josh's farm. What crops are grown in each field?

Josh and his dad walk in the fields to check the crops. "We look to see if any worms are eating the crops, or if there are weeds," says Josh.

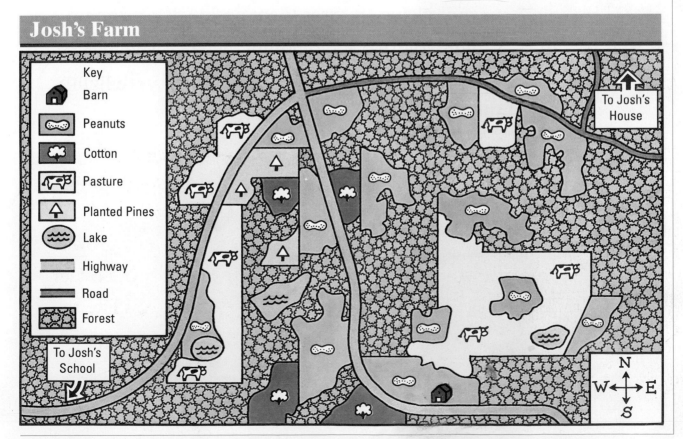

Josh's Farm

Key
- Barn
- Peanuts
- Cotton
- Pasture
- Planted Pines
- Lake
- Highway
- Road
- Forest

To Josh's House

To Josh's School

In the fall, Josh likes to help **harvest,** or pick, the peanuts. Josh and his dad check the peanuts to see if they are ready to harvest. Peanuts grow underground, so Josh has to dig up a peanut plant.

"The peanuts are ready to pick when the insides of the peanut shells are dark," Josh explains.

Josh's dad uses special machines to harvest peanuts. The digger is a machine that digs up the peanut plants. It turns them upside down on the ground to dry. Later another machine, called a combine, cuts the peanuts off the plants. It dumps the peanuts into big wagons.

When the peanuts are harvested, Josh's dad sells them to a peanut sheller. The sheller uses machines to clean the peanuts and to take off their shells. Then the sheller sells many of the peanuts to peanut butter factories. A **factory** is a place where something is made using machines.

Lots of people work in peanut butter factories. People run machines that roast the peanuts and grind them up into peanut butter. Other people use machines to fill the jars with peanut butter.

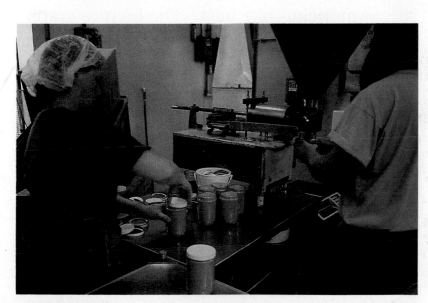

Even after the peanut butter is made, many more people work to bring it to you. Workers put the jars in boxes. Then they put the boxes into trucks. Truck drivers take the boxes to stores. Store workers take the jars out of boxes and place the jars of peanut butter on shelves.

Peanut butter is one of the foods Americans like best. The picture graph shows how much peanut butter a person eats. How much more peanut butter does a person eat now than 20 years ago?

Peanut Butter

How much does a person eat in one year?	
20 years ago	
Today	

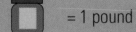 = 1 pound

The peanut butter in your next sandwich might be made from peanuts grown on Josh's farm. Josh's family grows enough peanuts to make almost nine million peanut butter sandwiches every year! A lot of people depend on one peanut farmer.

You depend on many people to make peanut butter. The next time you take a bite out of a peanut butter sandwich, remember to say "Thanks!"

REVIEW

1. What kinds of work do people do to make peanut butter?
2. How do the people in this lesson depend on machines to help them with their work?
3. How do people depend on each other to make peanut butter?
4. Look at the map on pages 182 and 183. Find Alabama. What states are close to Alabama?

Looking at the World

Josh and his family grow peanuts in the United States. People grow peanuts in other parts of the world, too. This is a world map. It shows the United States and many other places.

Look at the globe in your classroom. A globe is round like the earth. Look at the map. It shows the same thing as the globe, but the map is flat.

World Map

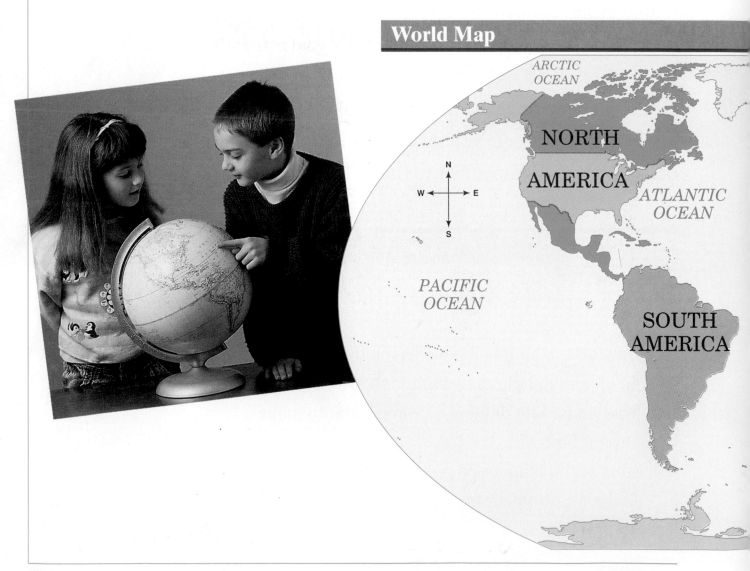

The map and the globe show where land and water are on the earth. On this map, thc water is blue. Different colors are used to show the land. The large pieces of land are called **continents.** The earth has seven continents. The names of the continents are on the map. What are they?

Around the continents is water. Each large area, or body, of water is an **ocean.** Find the names of the oceans on the map.

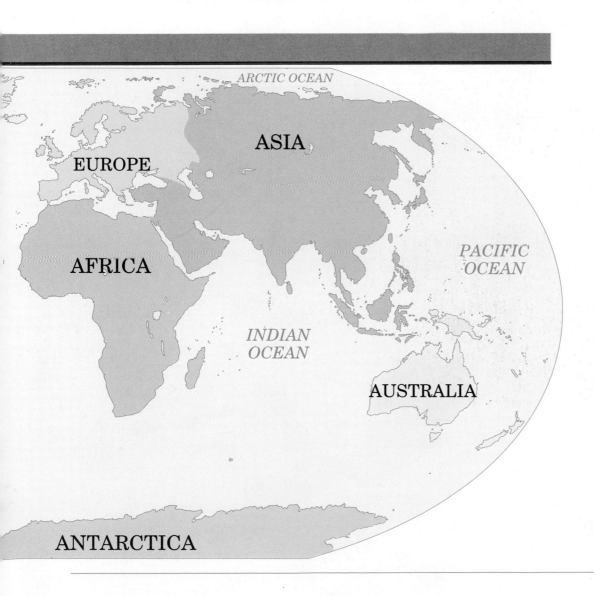

The map on this page shows the continent of North America. Most continents have many countries. People who live together in one **country** have the same leaders. They obey the same laws. Thick lines on this map divide one country from another.

North America

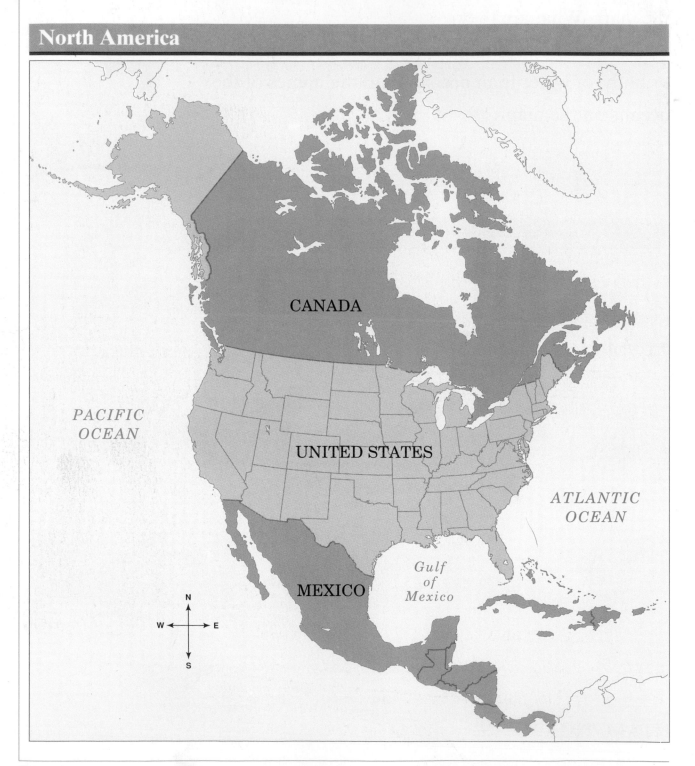

PACIFIC
OCEAN

CANADA

UNITED STATES

ATLANTIC
OCEAN

MEXICO

Gulf
of
Mexico

N
W — E
S

Most of the United States is on the continent of North America. One part of the United States, Hawaii, is not on this map because it is not on the continent of North America. Hawaii is a group of islands in the Pacific Ocean.

Other countries besides the United States are on the continent of North America. Look at the map on page 16. What country is north of the United States? What country is south?

Think about where you live. You live on the earth. On what continent do you live? In what country do you live? What is the name of your community?

Try It!

Find where you live on a map or globe. Do you live near an ocean or far from one? Do you live near Canada or Mexico? Tell where in the United States you live.

Where Food Comes From

You found out where peanut butter comes from. Now you can find out where stores get other foods, too.

Get Ready

1. Talk about where you think other foods come from.
2. Get paper, a pencil, crayons, and yarn.

Find Out

1. Look at the diagram. See where the food comes from.
2. Find out where other foods come from. Look at labels on boxes and cans of food. Talk to people. Use other books, too.

Where Does Your Food Come From?

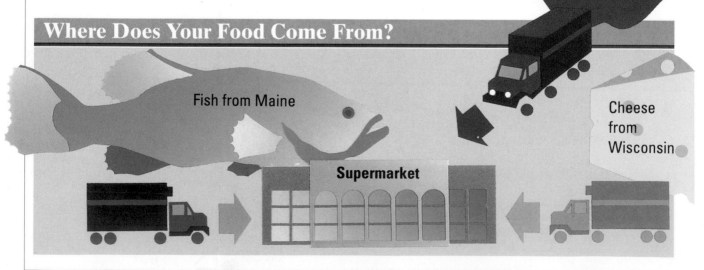

Apples from Washington

Fish from Maine

Cheese from Wisconsin

Supermarket

Move Ahead

1. Show where you live on a large map of the United States.

2. Use yarn to show where foods come from.

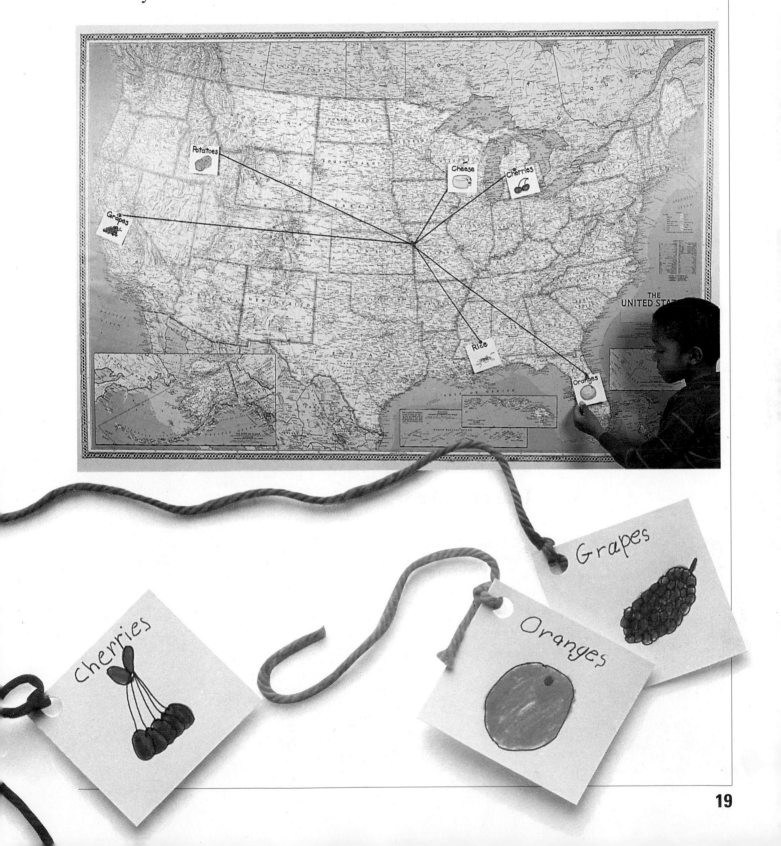

The Banana Bunch

THINK

How do bananas get from where they are grown to your lunch box?

Key Words

weather
seaport
route

Most of your food is grown by farmers here in the United States. But some food is grown far away. Many of the bananas you eat are grown in Honduras, a country south of the United States. These bananas must travel thousands of miles to reach you.

Honduras has the perfect weather for growing bananas. **Weather** is what the air is like—hot or cold, wet or dry. Bananas need hot sunshine and lots of rain, all year long. Weather in the United States is not good for growing bananas.

How are bananas harvested?

Bananas are grown on large farms called banana plantations.

Banana workers live and work on the plantation. Some of them take care of the banana plants. The workers protect the plants from bugs and weeds.

The banana workers must work in pairs to harvest the green bananas. One worker cuts the stems. The other worker carries the heavy bananas. He wears a shoulder pad to keep the bananas from getting bruised. He hooks the bananas to a moving cable that takes them to the packing plant.

What happens at the packing plant?

At the packing plant, workers cut bunches of bananas off the large stems. Other workers wash and weigh the bananas. Packers carefully place the bananas in boxes.

Then the boxes are put into containers, or large metal boxes. The containers keep the green bananas cool. If they get hot, the bananas may ripen and spoil before they get to your store.

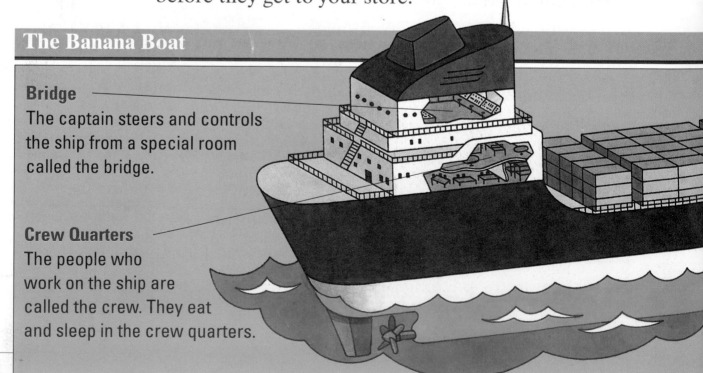

The Banana Boat

Bridge
The captain steers and controls the ship from a special room called the bridge.

Crew Quarters
The people who work on the ship are called the crew. They eat and sleep in the crew quarters.

How do bananas get to the United States?

The banana containers travel by train to Puerto Cortés, a seaport in Honduras. A **seaport** is a city by the sea. Seaports have docks that large ships can come to from the sea. Dock workers use cranes to lift the containers off the trains and into the waiting banana ship.

The captain gives the order for the ship to head out to sea. In less than a week, this ship will arrive at Gulfport, Mississippi, a seaport in the United States.

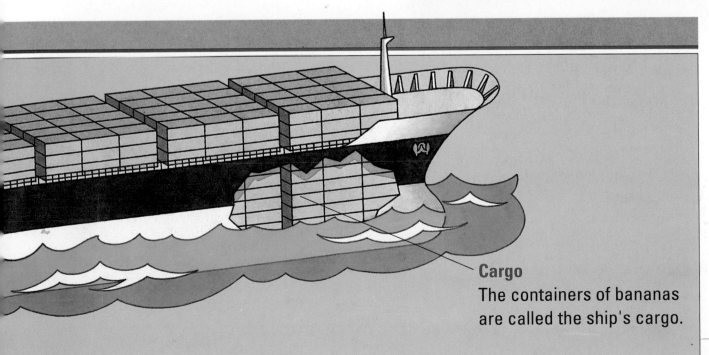

Cargo
The containers of bananas are called the ship's cargo.

The Banana Bunch Route

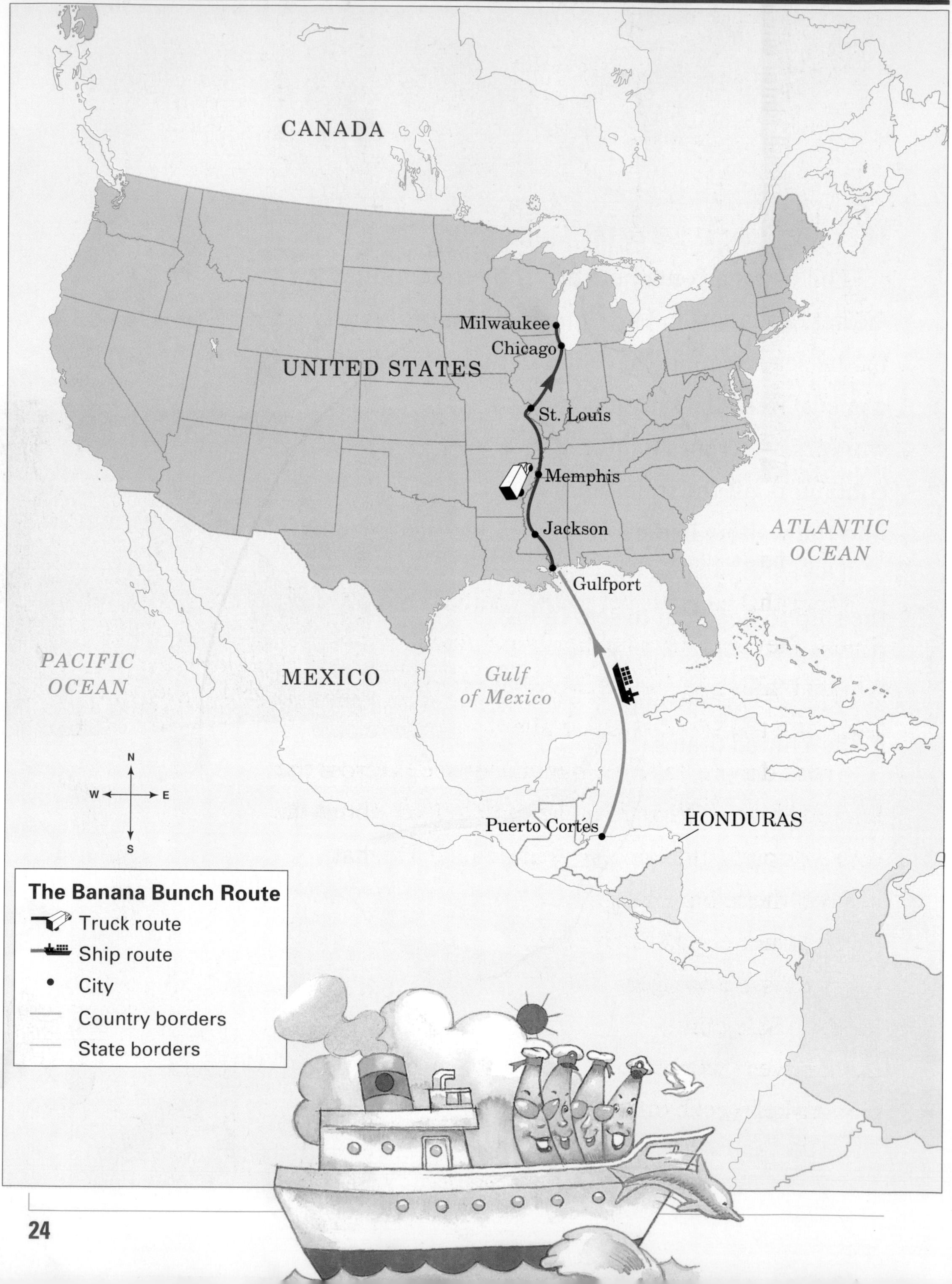

CANADA
UNITED STATES
MEXICO
HONDURAS
Milwaukee
Chicago
St. Louis
Memphis
Jackson
Gulfport
Puerto Cortés
ATLANTIC OCEAN
PACIFIC OCEAN
Gulf of Mexico
N
S
E
W
The Banana Bunch Route
Truck route
Ship route
City
Country borders
State borders

How do bananas get to the store?

Once the bananas get to the United States, they still have farther to go. Dock workers take the containers off the ship and place them onto truck trailers.

Truck drivers take the bananas to cities across the United States. What does the map tell you about the **route,** or path, the bananas will travel? To what city will these bananas go?

The truckers may drive for many days before they unload. Sometimes truck drivers work in pairs to help each other.

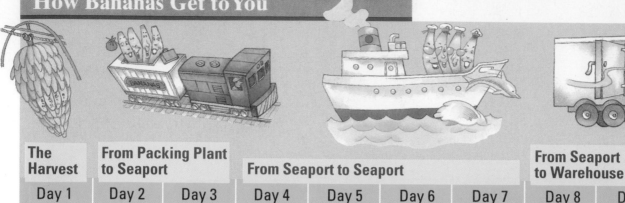

How Bananas Get to You

The Harvest	From Packing Plant to Seaport		From Seaport to Seaport				From Seaport to Warehouse	
Day 1	Day 2	Day 3	Day 4	Day 5	Day 6	Day 7	Day 8	Day 9

The truck drivers take the bananas to food warehouses. A food warehouse is a large building where many kinds of food are stored.

Most people do not want to buy green bananas. So when the boxes of bananas get to the warehouse, they are put in ripening rooms. The bananas start to turn yellow in these warm, wet rooms.

Storekeepers come to the food warehouse to buy bananas and other food for their stores.

					To Store	On Shelf in Store	
Ripening in Warehouse							
Day 10	Day 11	Day 12	Day 13	Day 14	Day 15	Day 16	Day 17	Day 18

At last! The bananas arrive at your store. It's been about two weeks since they were picked. Think about how far the bananas traveled by train, by ship, and by truck. Think of all the people along the route who worked to bring these bananas to you.

There they are, ready to be weighed and sold. Pick out a good bunch. Do you have your money? Pay the clerk.

Ummmm! Delicious!

REVIEW

1. How do bananas get from where they are grown to your lunch box?
2. What kinds of work do people do to bring bananas to you?
3. How is harvesting bananas different from harvesting peanuts?

27

You have learned that trucks carry bananas and other goods to all parts of the country. Now read an excerpt from a poem about busy truck drivers on the road.

LITERATURE

TRUCK SONG

Written by Diane Siebert

Illustrated by Byron Barton

at the truckstop
truckers meet
for road talk
and
a bite to eat
sipping coffee
hot and strong
jukebox plays
a country song

say good-bye
check your load
climb aboard
hit the road

heading out across the plains
checking mirrors, changing lanes
past the farms and fields of wheat
through the rain so cool and sweet
windshield wipers keeping time
lower gear to make the climb

up mountain roads
'round hairpin curves
with eagle eyes
and steely nerves

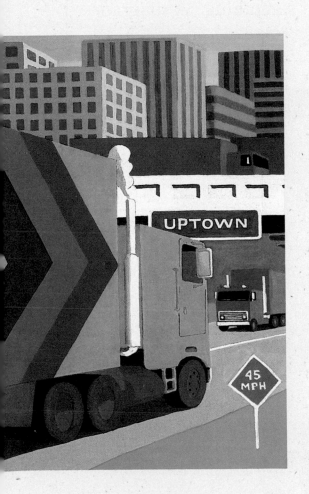

tractors pull
trailers full
deadlines must be met
journey's end
around the bend
gonna get there yet
off the freeway
into town
shifting
shifting
shifting
down

How Bananas Grow

You know what bananas look like. What do you know about the plants on which bananas grow?

Banana plants grow very tall. They may be 25 feet high. That is higher than your classroom ceiling! A banana plant does not have a trunk made of wood, as a tree does. A banana plant has a stalk made of leaves. The leaves wrap around each other.

Look at the drawing of the banana plant below. This kind of drawing is called a diagram. A **diagram** shows the important parts of something. A diagram also gives the names of these parts.

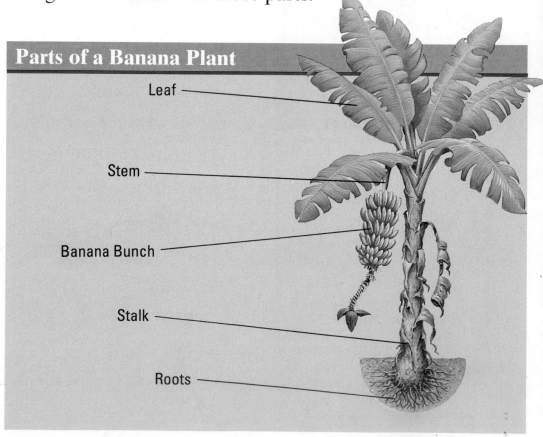

Parts of a Banana Plant

Leaf

Stem

Banana Bunch

Stalk

Roots

The diagram on page 34 shows where the leaves and stems are. It shows where the stalk and roots are, too. Find the banana bunch on the diagram.

Many plants start from seeds, but the banana plant does not. The diagrams below show how a new banana plant grows.

How a New Banana Plant Grows

Old Plant

New Growth

Old Plant

New Plant

Look at the first diagram. Find the old plant. Look at the tiny part underground that is growing out of the old plant. This new growth is the beginning of a new plant. What happens to this new growth in the second diagram?

Try It!

Make a diagram. Draw the tree shown at the right. In your drawing, show these tree parts: trunk, branches, leaves. Write the names of these parts, and show where they are.

Depending on Others

You depend on many people for your food. You also depend on people for other things. Think about your own city or town. Each person has a job. A city or town needs teachers, doctors, and fire fighters. It also needs dentists, gas-station owners, grocers, and many other workers. You depend on all these workers to do their jobs.

These workers also depend on one another. Look at the picture. Think about the ways that the people need one another.

Imagine a town or a city without these workers. What if there were no place to get gas for cars? How would fire fighters get to a fire? Where would everyone get food if there were no grocers? Who would teach the children if there were no teachers?

In every town or city, people depend on other people.

People Depend on You

THINK

How do food workers depend on you?

Key Word

consumer

Now you know that you depend on farmers, factory workers, truck drivers, and storekeepers for food. Did you know that *they* depend on *you,* too?

You buy peanut butter and bananas that they make and grow. A person who buys food and other goods is called a **consumer.** When you buy food, you are a consumer. Some of your money helps pay the people who worked hard to grow it,

pick it,

pack it,

ship it,

and sell it.

The people who work to bring you food depend on each other. Factory workers depend on farmers. Farmers depend on factory workers. Storekeepers depend on truck drivers. Truck drivers depend on storekeepers. And they all depend on consumers.

What would you do without all these people? What would they do without you?

REVIEW

1. How do food workers depend on you?
2. What is a consumer?
3. How do food workers depend on each other?

Unit 1 Review

Words

What words go in the blanks?

consumer
crops
depend
factory
harvest
route
seaport
weather

1. You _____ on farmers to grow your food.
2. In a ____ , people use machines to make things.
3. In the spring, farmers plant their ____ .
4. When you buy something, you are a ____ .
5. Bananas need hot ____ to grow.
6. A ____ is a city where ships unload their cargo.
7. Look on the map to find the shortest ____ from here to the library.
8. Farmers use special machines to ____ peanuts.

Ideas

1. What kinds of work do people do to bring you peanut butter? What do people do to bring you bananas?
2. How do all of these people depend on you?

Skills

1. Look at the map key on the next page. Find the symbol for the gas station. With your finger, trace a route on the map from the gas station to the school. Which direction did you travel first? Which direction did you travel next?

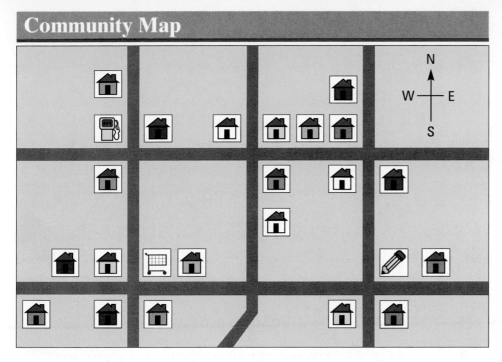

Community Map

Key

🅖 Gas Station

✏ School

🛒 Supermarket

🏠 House

2. Look at the world map on pages 180–181. Find the continent of North America. What countries are on this continent?

3. Find the Pacific Ocean on the world map. Name one continent it touches.

Activities

1. Work with your class to make a list of the people you depend on to bring bananas and peanut butter to your store. Draw pictures of these people. Help make a mural with the pictures.

2. Work with one or two other students to draw a map of an imaginary place such as an island or a castle. Include a map key for the map. Decide which direction is north. Then make a compass rose for your map.

Unit 2

Knowing Your Family

Grandpa tells me stories
About when he was small.
Aunt Jane sends me birthday cards,
And says I'm growing tall.

Mama says I look a lot
Like all the family.
I'm glad that I am part of them
And glad that I am me.

Learning About Ancestors

Key Word

ancestors

Are you tall or short? Is your hair curly or straight? Did you know that your looks come from your ancestors?

Your **ancestors** are all the people in your family, starting with your parents, who were born before you. Your sisters and brothers are not your ancestors. But your parents, grandparents, great-grandparents, and their parents, grandparents, and great-grandparents are all your ancestors.

You get many things from your ancestors besides the curl in your hair. You may have a smile or a laugh just like a great-grandparent.

Do you like looking like your ancestors? Here is what one person says!

▲ *The great-grandmother in this family picture is the ancestor of all the others.*

Everybody Says

Everybody says
I look just like my mother.
Everybody says
I'm the image of Aunt Bee.
Everybody says
My nose is like my father's,
But *I* want to look like *me*.

Dorothy Aldis

You learn many things from your ancestors, too. Parents and grandparents teach children what they think is important. They teach about sharing with others. They might tell children how important it is to work hard in school. What important things do your parents and grandparents teach you?

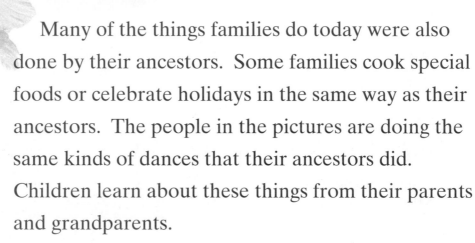

Many of the things families do today were also done by their ancestors. Some families cook special foods or celebrate holidays in the same way as their ancestors. The people in the pictures are doing the same kinds of dances that their ancestors did. Children learn about these things from their parents and grandparents.

Most people in the United States have ancestors who came from other countries. Some ancestors moved here long, long ago, and others have just moved here. Ancestors of Native Americans came here long before any of the others.

Everyone has ancestors. The chart below shows how one girl is related to some of her ancestors.

In the next five lessons, you will read about some real children and their families. These five families may be a lot like your family, or they may be very different.

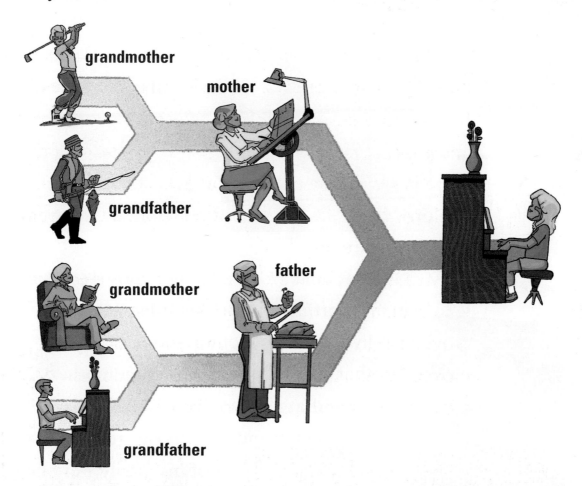

grandmother

mother

grandfather

grandmother

father

grandfather

R E V I E W

1. How are your ancestors important to you?
2. Who are a person's ancestors?
3. What are some things you get from your ancestors?

Coming from Cambodia

THINK

What did the Suos family have to learn when they moved to the United States?

Key Word

holiday

The Suos family in Boston

Roattanak *(RAH tuh nahk)* Suos *(SOOS)* lives in an apartment in Boston, Massachusetts. He lives with his mother and father, his brother, and his sister. His grandmother and grandfather also live with him.

Roattanak and his sister were born in the United States. Most of his family were born in Cambodia. Look at the map on the next page. Find Cambodia.

In Boston, Roattanak can play in the snow in the winter. He could not do that in Cambodia. It never snows there.

Life in Cambodia

The weather in Cambodia is always hot, and it rains often. People do not wear heavy clothing. Both men and women often wear sarongs, a kind of skirt made from brightly colored cloth. A sarong would not keep you warm in Boston in winter!

In Cambodia, Roattanak's father lived with his family in the city of Phnom Penh *(puh NAHM PEHN)*. There were not many cars there. Most people traveled on bicycles. Even taxi drivers drove three-wheeled bicycles that looked like giant tricycles!

49

A favorite
Cambodian food

Phnom Penh is often called "the city of holidays." A **holiday** is a day to celebrate someone or something special. Roattanak's father remembers how he celebrated New Year's Day. It is one of the most important holidays in Cambodia. New Year's Day is in April in Cambodia, not on January 1 as it is in the United States. On New Year's Day, Roattanak's father sang and danced and ate special foods. He played games with the other boys and girls.

The Cambodian Royal Ballet dances at the Royal Palace in Phnom Penh.

Roattanak's grandparents, parents, brother, and their friends before his family moved to Boston

Life in the United States

Roattanak's parents and grandparents left Cambodia because of a terrible war. They decided to come to the United States.

At first, living in Boston was not easy for Roattanak's family. Imagine going to a place where you could not understand anything people said. Imagine not knowing how to shop for food, how to turn the lights on or off, or how to read the signs. That's what happened to Roattanak's parents.

For Roattanak's family, everything in the United States was strange. They didn't know about supermarkets. In Cambodia, fresh food was sold in outdoor markets.

In Cambodia, people shopped every day for just enough food for that day. How often does your family shop for food?

The money was new to Roattanak's family, too. The coins and dollars in this country are different from Cambodian money. Why do you think a different kind of money would make shopping hard?

"How do we turn off the lights?" they wondered. In Cambodia there were no wall switches. Instead, people pulled cords.

Our alphabet is not the same as they use in Cambodia. Roattanak's father studied hard to learn to read, write, and speak English.

Words from Cambodia

Looks Like	Sounds Like	Means
ឈប់	(ZHAHP)	stop
គ្រូ	(GROO)	teacher
កូនស្រី	(koon SREE)	girl
កូនប្រុស	(koon PROO)	boy

Now Roattanak's family enjoys life in the United States. They go to the beach together in the summer. Roattanak's grandfather still likes to go shopping for food every day.

Roattanak's parents talk about life in Cambodia. They remind everyone in the family about things that are important to them. Showing good manners and working hard in school are some of those things. Roattanak is learning about the good things from both countries.

REVIEW

1. What did the Suos family have to learn when they moved to the United States?
2. What special things did people do in the city of Phnom Penh?
3. How was life in Cambodia different from life in the United States?

Take a Good Look

You have read about two cities—Boston and Phnom Penh. These two cities are *alike* in some ways. They are *different* in other ways.

What is one way that Boston and Phnom Penh are alike? They are both big cities. What is one way that they are different? The streets of Boston are filled with cars. The streets of Phnom Penh are filled with bicycles.

Look at the pictures below and read about Lak and Katie. How are Lak and Katie alike? How are they different?

▲ *Katie is eight years old.*
She wears a shirt and pants.

▲ *Lak is eight years old.*
She wears a sarong.

When you read or look at pictures, you will find ways that places and people are alike and different.

Try It!

Look at the pictures below, and read the sentences. How are the places alike? How are the places different?

◄ *People shop at a supermarket in Boston.*

◄ *People shop at an outdoor market in Phnom Penh.*

Two Countries, Two Traditions

THINK

What traditions does Teresa celebrate?

Key Words

history
tradition

Imagine living in the same house where your grandmother grew up. Teresa Sanchez does. She lives in the house where her grandmother *and* her mother grew up. She even goes to the same school they went to.

Teresa's family has lived in East Los Angeles, California, for a long time. Their ancestors came from Mexico. Teresa and her family speak Spanish, the language of Mexico. They also speak English. They eat foods from the United States and Mexico. They enjoy the holidays of both countries, too.

Teresa and her cousin

56

Jalisco, Mexico

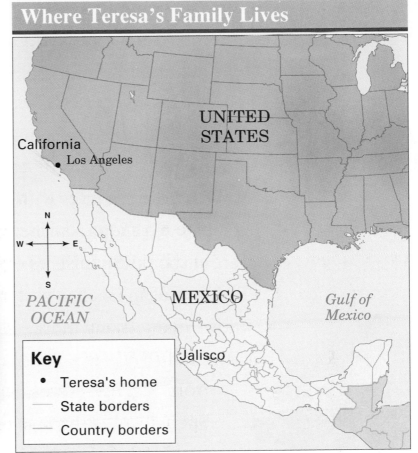

UNITED STATES

California
● Los Angeles

N
W ← → E
S

PACIFIC OCEAN

MEXICO

Gulf of Mexico

Jalisco

Key
● Teresa's home
⋯⋯ State borders
— Country borders

Teresa's father came to the United States when he was 22 years old. He came from the Mexican state of Jalisco (*huh LEES koh*). Today, her father works as a carpet layer in California. Teresa's Grandpa Sanchez and other members of her family still live in Mexico.

Most of Teresa's ancestors were farmers in Mexico. They lived in green valleys with mountains all around. Teresa's Grandpa Sanchez is still a farmer.

▼ *Drawings like this were put on bowls made in Jalisco.*

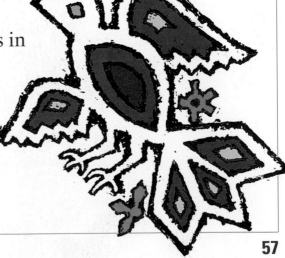

Teresa's Two Languages

When Teresa and her Grandpa Sanchez visit, he tells her about what happened long ago when he was a boy. He tells Teresa about her family's history. **History** is all the things that have happened in the past.

When Teresa talks with her grandpa, they speak Spanish. Grandpa Sanchez does not speak English. Teresa speaks Spanish *and* English. Here are words Teresa uses in English and in Spanish. Of course, she knows many, many more. How many do you know?

Teresa's Two Languages

Spanish		English
niña *(NEEN yah)*		girl
casa *(CA sah)*		house
niño *(NEEN yoh)*		boy
libro *(LEE broh)*		book
gato *(GAH toh)*		cat
fruta *(FROO tah)*		fruit

Teresa's Two Kinds of Foods

Teresa's family enjoys food from both countries. Some nights her family eats hamburgers on buns. Other nights they eat Mexican rice with their meals.

Having special foods on holidays is a tradition in Teresa's family. A **tradition** is something that is done a certain way for many years. Teresa's grandmother makes buñuelos *(boon WAY lohs)* for New Year's Day. Buñuelos are a tradition of Mexico. They are small pieces of dough that are fried. After Grandmother cooks the dough, she mixes sugar and cinnamon together and sprinkles it on top. Sometimes she makes a syrup with cinnamon and sugar, too. It tastes good!

Buñuelos

1. Mix

2. Shape

3. Fry

4. Sprinkle

Teresa's Two Sets of Holidays

Teresa celebrates two sets of holidays. On September 15 and 16, her family celebrates Mexican Independence. During this holiday, it is a tradition to have fiestas *(fee EHS tuhs)*. Fiestas are like fairs or big picnics. These pictures show what Teresa might see at a fiesta. People wear colorful clothes. They dance and eat special foods and play games.

Teresa's family also celebrates Thanksgiving and the Fourth of July. These holidays are traditions of the United States.

Many of Teresa's neighbors and classmates have ancestors from **Mexico**. In school, they learn about the history and holidays of both countries.

Teresa's family knows two languages and celebrates two sets of holidays. They feel lucky to have the traditions of two countries.

REVIEW

1. What traditions does Teresa celebrate?
2. What are some ways Teresa's family keeps the traditions of two countries?
3. What are some important traditions in your family?

What Do You Do?

Teresa and her family have both Mexican and American traditions. Some of their traditions are the foods they eat and the holidays they celebrate.

How you celebrate your birthday is a tradition. Having a cake with a candle for each year of age is an American tradition. Not everyone celebrates birthdays in the same way, though. Let's look at some of the different ways people around the world celebrate birthdays.

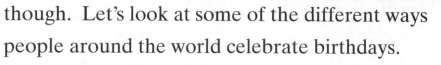

People in Denmark hang flags outside their homes on their birthdays. In Russia, people celebrate their birthdays with a birthday pie.

Поздравление

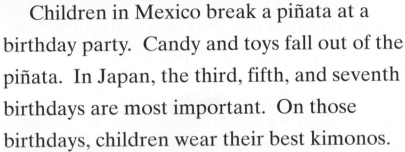

Children in Mexico break a piñata at a birthday party. Candy and toys fall out of the piñata. In Japan, the third, fifth, and seventh birthdays are most important. On those birthdays, children wear their best kimonos.

Many other things are traditions. For example, the Christmas tree is a tradition that came from Germany. Having turkey on Thanksgiving is a tradition that started in America.

A tradition is something that is done a certain way for many years. A family passes on traditions to the children. Everyone has traditions. Think about some of the traditions in your family.

Life Long Ago

THINK

What does David
know about his
ancestors?

Key Word

suburb

David Schweizer (*SHWEYE zur*) lives in a suburb near Chicago, Illinois. A **suburb** is a community near a big city. David lives on a quiet street with lots of trees. He can walk to school because it is near his house. Before school, David likes to play with his computer. After school, he plays with his friends who live nearby.

David likes living in his community. He has lived there all of his life. His ancestors, however, have lived in many different places.

David and
his sister

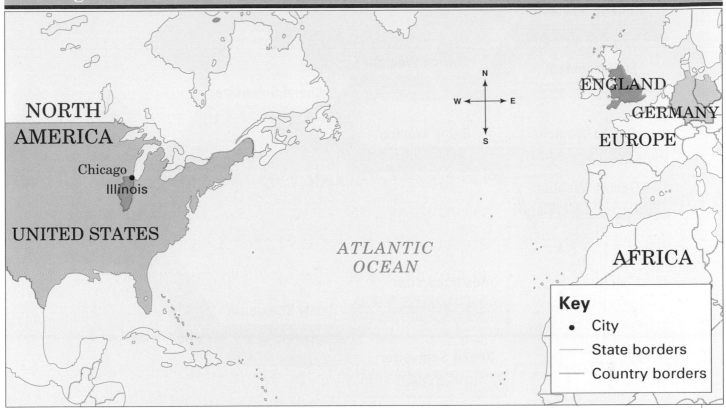

NORTH
AMERICA

Chicago
Illinois

UNITED STATES

ATLANTIC
OCEAN

ENGLAND
GERMANY
EUROPE

AFRICA

Key
- • City
- — State borders
- — Country borders

Great-grandmother Neustadt

David's Great-grandmother Hedwig Neustadt
(NOY shtaht) was born in Germany. When she was
nine years old, she moved to the United States. Her
father had heard good things about the United States.
He decided to leave Germany
and move here.

Hedwig's father didn't have
the money to bring all of his
family at once. He came from
Germany by himself. When
he got here, he earned money
by working for a farmer.
When he had saved enough
money, he sent for his family.

Hedwig with her family

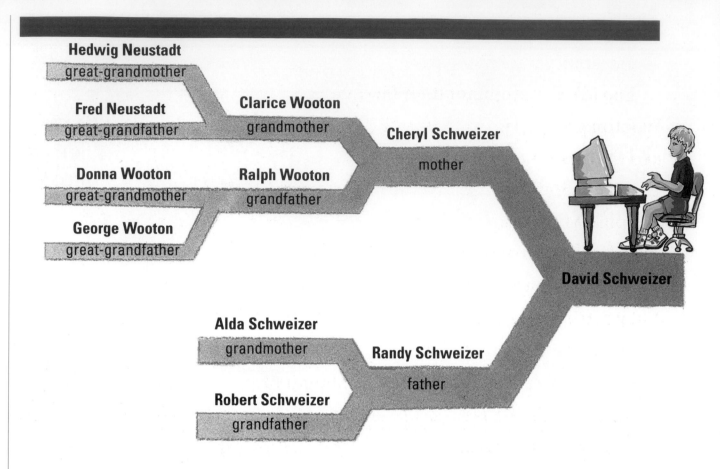

Hedwig Neustadt
great-grandmother

Fred Neustadt
great-grandfather

Clarice Wooton
grandmother

Donna Wooton
great-grandmother

Ralph Wooton
grandfather

George Wooton
great-grandfather

Cheryl Schweizer
mother

David Schweizer

Alda Schweizer
grandmother

Randy Schweizer
father

Robert Schweizer
grandfather

Hedwig, her brothers and sisters, and her mother came to the United States on a boat. They landed at a place called Ellis Island in New York Harbor.

Hedwig went to school and learned English. When she was only twelve, she left school to go to work. She had to earn money to help her family. In those days, many children worked. Hedwig loved to read, and she taught herself many things.

When Hedwig grew up, she married Fred Neustadt. They lived on a farm. Their daughter Clarice is now David's grandmother.

Great-grandmother Hedwig Neustadt

Great-grandfather Wooton

David's Great-grandfather George Wooton grew up in Arkansas. Long ago the Wooton ancestors came from England. Some settled on a farm near Flippin, Arkansas.

When David's Great-grandfather Wooton got married, he and his wife decided to move. They settled near Binger, Oklahoma. That was long before there were cars. They traveled in a covered wagon. It took 22 days to get from Flippin to Binger. Today you can travel the same distance in a car in about one day.

Flippin, Arkansas, to Binger, Oklahoma: How Long Would It Take?	
Covered Wagon	22 days
Train	3 days
Car	1 day
Plane	1 hour

▲ *David's great-grandparents took these pots with them in the covered wagon.*

David's great-grandparents missed the green hills and clear streams of Arkansas. So after one year, they went back to live on a farm near Flippin.

In those days, farmers did not have machines to help them with their work. Instead they used horses and mules. Great-grandfather Wooton owned a team of mules. One was black and one was red. Great-grandfather Wooton worked with the mules to plant corn, cut hay, and carry wood for the family's cooking stove.

Their son Ralph grew up on the farm near Flippin. He is now David's grandpa.

David's great-grandparents with their family

David's mother, Cheryl, and her brother, when they were children

When Ralph Wooton met and married Clarice Neustadt, they settled in Missouri where they still live. Their daughter, Cheryl, is David's mother.

David likes to visit his grandparents. They live on the same street where David's mother grew up. When David visits, his grandpa takes him fishing. Sometimes he tells David how his ancestors lived.

REVIEW

1. What does David know about his ancestors?
2. How was Great-grandmother Neustadt's life different from David's life?
3. How do think your life is different from the lives of your ancestors?

Finding Your Way

David's ancestors grew up on farms. They had to travel far to visit people or to go to a store. David lives in a suburb. Homes and stores are closer together.

Look at the map on the next page. It shows David's neighborhood. Find David's house on the map. Find the library. How could David go to the library? Trace a route with your finger.

The streets on the map divide the map into blocks. The streets form a grid on the map. A **grid** divides a map into small squares.

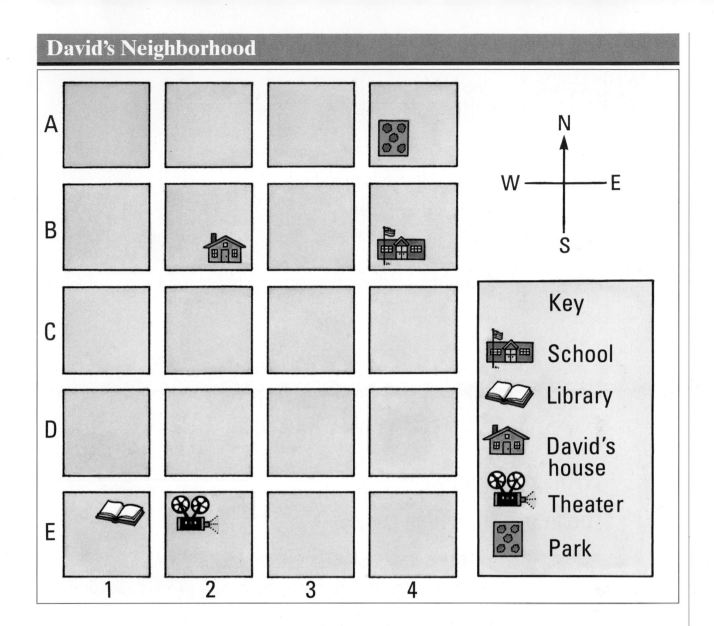

A grid on a map makes it easier to find places. Find the letters along the left side of the map. Then find the numbers along the bottom of the map.

The school is in square B4. Put your finger on the letter B. Move it across the squares until you are in the row above the number 4. That is square B4.

Try It!

Use the map above. What is in square E1? What is in square E2? In what square is the park?

You have been reading about all sorts of families. Many of the families had an ancestor who came from another country. In this story, a little girl tells about when her great-grandmother came to America.

WATCH THE STARS COME OUT

Written by Riki Levinson

Illustrated by Diane Goode

Grandma told me when her Mama was a little girl she had red hair—just like me.

Grandma's Mama loved to go to bed early and watch the stars come out—just like me.

Every Friday night, after the dishes were put away, Grandma's Mama would come to her room and tell her a special story.

When I was a little girl, my big Brother
and I went on a big boat to America.
Mama and Papa and Sister were waiting
there for us.

My aunt, Mama's sister, took us to the
boat. She didn't bring my two little
brothers. They were too small. They would
come on a boat when they were older.

Aunt gave us a barrel full of dried fruit. She asked an old lady to watch over us. And she did. She also ate our dried fruit.

The old lady and Brother and I went down the steps to our room. I counted the steps as we carried our bundles down, but there were so many, I forgot to count after a while.

Sometimes the boat rocked back and forth—it was fun! Some people didn't like it—they got sick. The old lady got very, very sick. She died.

Brother told me not to worry. He would take care of me—he was ten.

At night when I went to sleep, I couldn't see the stars come out in the sky. That made me sad.

Each morning when we got up, Brother put a mark on his stick. I counted them—twenty-three.

The last morning we looked across the water. There were two islands near each other. One of them had a statue standing on it—a lady with a crown. Everyone got very excited and waved to her. I did too.

When the boat stopped, we carried our bundles down the plank.

I started to cry. I did not see Mama and Papa and Sister. A sailor told me not to worry—we would see them soon.

We went on another boat to a place on an island.

We carried our bundles into a big, big room. Brother and I went into a small room with all the other children without mamas and papas.

A lady looked at me all over. I wondered why.

I waited for Brother. The lady looked at him too.

The next day we went on a
ferry. The land came closer
and closer as we watched.
Everyone waved. We did too.
Mama and Papa and Sister
were there!

We went on a trolley to our home. Mama
said it was a palace.

Mama's palace was on the top floor. I
counted the steps as we walked up—fifty-two!

Mama and Papa's room was in the middle.
Our room was in the front. And in the back
was the kitchen with a big black stove.

Mama warmed a big pot of water on the
stove. She poured some into the sink and
helped me climb in to wash.

Mama washed my hair, and
when it was dry, she brushed it.
It felt good.

Sister gave us cookies and
glasses of tea.

I was very tired.

I kissed Mama and Sister good-night. Papa patted me on my head and said I was his little princess.

I went into our room and climbed into Sister's bed. It was right next to the window.

I watched the stars come out. One, two, three.

This Friday night I will go to bed very early and watch the stars come out in the sky.

I hope Grandma will come to my room and tell me another special story.

What to Bring

David's ancestors came to the United States from far away. When they came, they had to decide what to bring along. They couldn't bring everything.

Long ago, many families moved to the United States with only a few suitcases or trunks. They packed just the clothes they needed. Many people also brought a few special pictures and family treasures.

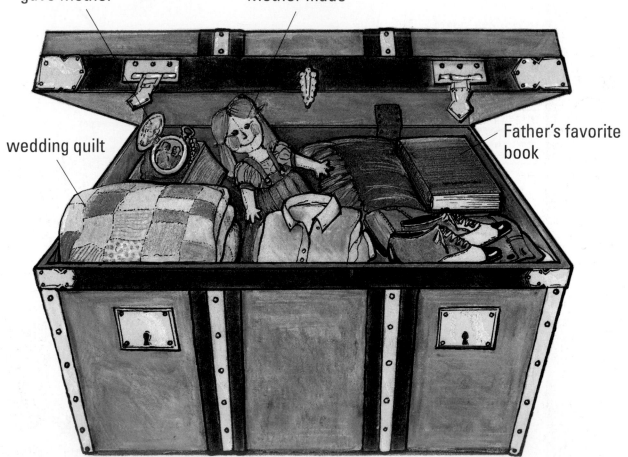

locket that Grandfather gave Mother

doll that Mother made

wedding quilt

Father's favorite book

Imagine that you are moving and can only bring along one suitcase. What will you pack in it?

Think about what you will need. You will need clothes, of course. Which ones will you pack? What else is really important to you? Will it fit in your suitcase?

Look at the pictures. Think about what you will bring and what you will leave behind.

Make a list of the things that you will bring. Remember, all the things must fit in one suitcase. Tell why you chose each.

Life Then and Now

THINK

How is David's life different from his ancestors' lives?

Key Word

education

Meet David Winslow. He is in second grade, and he lives with his mother, his father, and his sister. They live in a suburb near St. Louis, Missouri.

David stays in an after-school program while his parents work. He goes on field trips and plays games with the other children.

When he is not in school, David likes to play T-ball, baseball, and especially soccer. He also likes to play video games and to build model cars and airplanes.

Winslow Childhood Homes

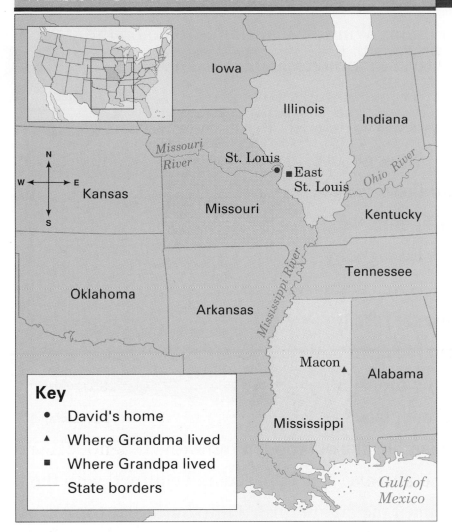

Key
- **●** David's home
- **▲** Where Grandma lived
- **■** Where Grandpa lived
- — State borders

Grandma Winslow

When David's grandparents were children, life was different for them. Grandma Winslow grew up on a farm near Macon, Mississippi. She had nine brothers and four sisters. There was a lot of hard work on the farm, but there was also time to play.

Grandma Winslow did not buy toys at the store. She thought of ways to make her own toys. If she wanted to make a playhouse, she used boxes. If she wanted to play jacks, she used a big rock for a ball and smaller rocks for jacks.

Grandma Winslow had chores to do on the farm. Every morning she had to churn cream to make butter. To churn means to stir very hard. First, one of her brothers milked the cows. Then the milk was left out all night in a bowl. The cream in the milk rose to the top.

In the morning, Grandma placed the cream in a large wooden tub with a long stick in it. She churned and churned with the stick until the cream turned into butter. It took a long time, and Grandma's arms got tired. Grandma loved the farm, but she did not like to churn.

Crops growing in Mississippi

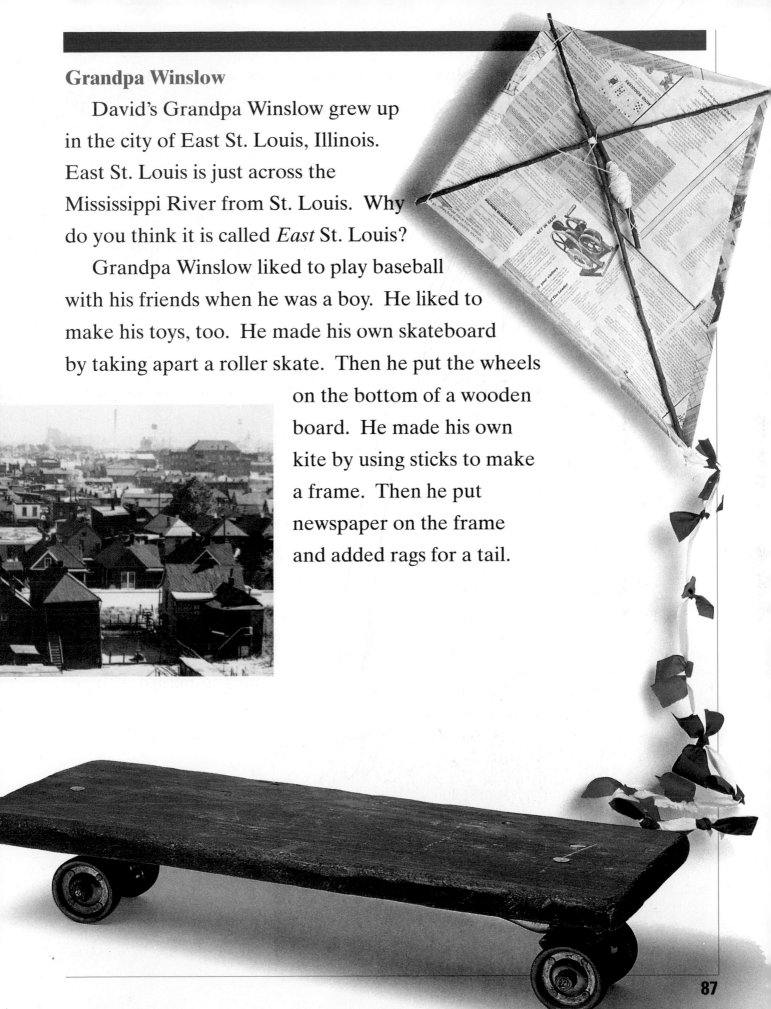

Grandpa Winslow

David's Grandpa Winslow grew up in the city of East St. Louis, Illinois. East St. Louis is just across the Mississippi River from St. Louis. Why do you think it is called *East* St. Louis?

Grandpa Winslow liked to play baseball with his friends when he was a boy. He liked to make his toys, too. He made his own skateboard by taking apart a roller skate. Then he put the wheels on the bottom of a wooden board. He made his own kite by using sticks to make a frame. Then he put newspaper on the frame and added rags for a tail.

David Today

David's life is different from the lives of his ancestors. In some ways, though, he is a lot like them. His father and grandfather love sports. So does David.

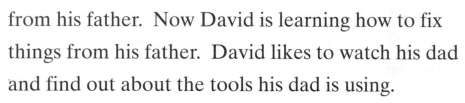

David's father learned to fix things and build things from his father. Now David is learning how to fix things from his father. David likes to watch his dad and find out about the tools his dad is using.

David is learning how important education is, too. Getting an **education** means going to school to learn ideas, facts, or skills. David's mother finished her college education when David was a baby. That was hard work, but getting an education was very important to her.

David's parents want him and his sister to go to college, too.

Together, David and his parents learn about the history of other Americans like themselves. They are proud of the people who worked to make life better.

One of the best things David has learned from his ancestors is the importance of his family. The chart below shows the names of some of David's ancestors.

Hattie Payne
grandmother

Lee Payne Jr.
grandfather

Brenda Winslow
mother

David Anson Winslow II

Odell Winslow
grandmother

David Anson Winslow
father

Homer Winslow
grandfather

REVIEW

1. How is David's life different from his ancestors' lives?
2. How is David like his ancestors?
3. What are some games or toys that you could make?

A Long Time Here

In beauty, I shall walk.
In beauty, you shall be my picture.
In beauty, you shall be my song.

from the Navajo Nightway Ceremony

THINK

What traditions has Melanie learned from her family?

Key Word

weave

This poem is about the land where Melanie Begaye *(beh GAY)* lives. Melanie is eight years old. She lives with her family near Round Rock, Arizona. Her ancestors have lived on this land for many years, since before the United States became a country. Melanie and her family are Navajos.

The land where Melanie lives is beautiful, but little rain falls there. Sometimes people have to bring water from far away. There is little grass. The land is tan and brown with big red rocks.

There are no big cities near where Melanie lives. There are no tall buildings. Melanie can look out across the land and see for a long way. She can see mountains in the distance.

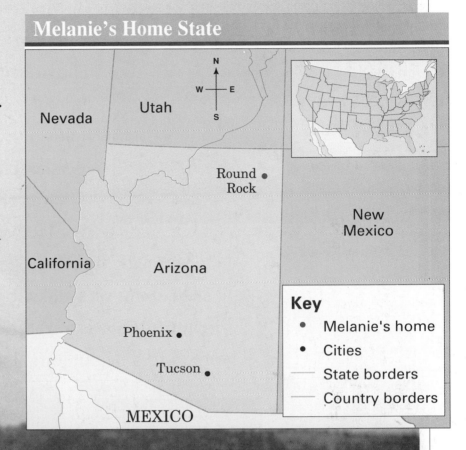

Melanie's Home State

Nevada

Utah

Round Rock

New Mexico

California

Arizona

Phoenix

Tucson

MEXICO

Key
- Melanie's home
- Cities
- ⋯⋯ State borders
- — Country borders

When Melanie gets home from school, she rides her horse, Streak. She has been riding horses since she was three. Melanie rides her bike, too.

Melanie likes to visit her grandparents who live nearby. They raise sheep and other animals. Sometimes Melanie helps her Grandma Nez herd the sheep.

Grandma Nez uses the sheep's wool to weave rugs. To **weave** means to lace threads together to make cloth. It takes about six weeks to make a rug. Weaving beautiful rugs is a tradition among Navajo women that began long, long ago.

The designs used for the rugs are not written down. The weavers keep them in their minds and teach them to their daughters.

Some weavers buy the thread, but some like to make their own. They shear, or cut, the wool off the sheep.

Weavers clean the wool and twist it into thread.

Sometimes weavers use dyes that they buy in the store to color the thread. Sometimes they make their own dyes from plants. This color was made from the juniper bush.

This color was made from onion skins.

Melanie's Aunt Lucy weaves, too. In this picture, Aunt Lucy is just beginning to weave a rug.

Melanie learns other things from her family. During the winter, Melanie's grandparents like to tell stories. After supper, when the sun sets, the family sits around the fire. Melanie's grandparents tell about the smart coyote who is always playing tricks on others. Coyote stories are a tradition with the Navajo people.

Melanie has learned many family traditions. She has learned to share and to care for others. She often takes care of her little brother, Merrell. She has learned to share food and clothes with people who need them.

Melanie has also learned to understand and to speak some Navajo words. She has learned to care for sheep. Her grandparents have taught her coyote stories. Someday, she may teach all these things to her grandchildren.

REVIEW

1. What traditions has Melanie learned from her family?
2. Where do Melanie's grandma and Aunt Lucy get their rug designs?
3. The picture on pages 90–91 shows the land where Melanie lives. Draw a picture of the things around your home.

Working and Sharing

One Navajo custom Melanie learned is to share with others. When working on a school project, everyone should share, too.

People working as a group share things such as scissors and glue. They also share their ideas. They learn from each other, and they help each other. Everyone has a chance to have an important part.

Read the list below. It tells what to do when you work in a group.

1. Tell the others your ideas about the project.

2. Listen to the ideas of others.

3. Help to do the work.

These children are working on a paper Navajo rug. They all planned the design of the rug. Each person had a chance to talk while others listened. Now they are making the rug. They are sharing their ideas with each other. Everyone helps to make the rug beautiful.

Try It!

You can work with others to make a paper rug. Work with two or three other students. Here is how:

1. Choose a shape to place on the rug. It could be a circle, a square, or a simple animal drawing. Draw the shape. Make it an easy shape to cut out.

2. Decide as a group how to make the rug design. Use the shapes from all of the people in your group. Repeat each one many times to make the design. Share ideas.

3. Work together to make the paper rug.

Unit 2 Review

Words

Match each word with its meaning.

ancestors
education
history
holiday
suburb
tradition
weave

1. All your family, starting with your parents, who were born before you
2. To lace threads together to make cloth
3. A community near a big city
4. A day to celebrate something or someone special
5. All the things that have happened in the past
6. To learn ideas, facts, or skills
7. Something done a certain way for many years

Ideas

1. Make a list of things people might have to learn when they move to a different country.
2. Tell some of the ways life was different for children long ago than it is for children today.
3. Teresa Sanchez and Melanie Begaye learned many traditions from their families. Tell about some of the traditions they learned.

Skills

1. Look at the pictures on the next page. Tell how the places are alike. Tell how they are different.

On a farm

In the city

2. Look at the grid on the map. Put your finger on the letter B. Move your finger along the square to row 2. What is the name of that square?

3. In what grid square is the library?

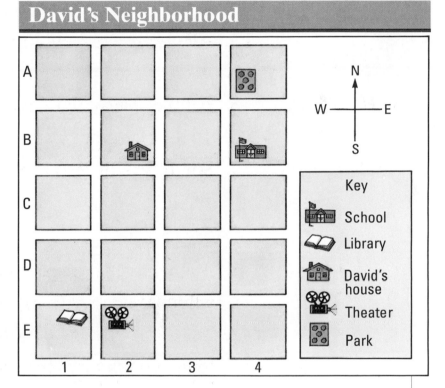

David's Neighborhood

Key

School
Library
David's house
Theater
Park

Activities

1. Work with one or two other students. Make a list of things people get from their ancestors. Make a poster that shows these things.

2. Work with your class to make a list of where all the ancestors in these lessons came from. Find these places on the world map in your classroom.

Unit 3

Living in Our Country

My country is a special place
And means so much to me.
It's where I live and play and learn
With friends and family.

Symbols and celebrations
Are ways we show our pride
In how this special nation
Makes us feel inside.

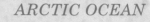

ARCTIC OCEAN

We Are One Country

Countries come in all shapes and sizes. We live in a country called the United States of America. Our country is made up of 50 states. Most of them are grouped together in one area, but two are far away—Alaska and Hawaii. Alaska is in the north. Hawaii is a group of islands. It is in the Pacific Ocean.

All the states together make one country. Find the United States of America on the map.

PACIFIC OCEAN

CANADA

UNITED STATES

ATLANTIC OCEAN

MEXICO

Gulf of Mexico

— Country borders
— State borders

Our country is like a big family. How many people are in your family? Two? Three? Four or more? Imagine a family with millions of people in it.

Our country is made up of millions of citizens. A **citizen** is a person who belongs to a country. Both children and grownups are citizens. The pictures on these pages show citizens of our country.

We don't all look alike. We don't all do the same work. We don't all agree on everything, either. But we are all citizens of one country—the United States.

As citizens of one country, we are alike in some ways. We have one flag. We have one President. We believe in many of the same things. One of the most important things we believe in is that all people should be free. What are other things that make us one country?

REVIEW

1. What makes us one country?
2. Who are citizens?
3. Ask some grownups what they like about being citizens of our country. Write down what they say.

We Celebrate Together

THINK

Why do people in our country celebrate holidays?

Key Words

celebrate
colony

Holidays are a part of our country's history. Each year we celebrate holidays together. To **celebrate** means to do special things with family and friends.

Why do we celebrate Thanksgiving?

The Pilgrims celebrated the first Thanksgiving in America. They left England to have their own kind of church. They sailed across the ocean and landed at a place they named Plymouth.

Pilgrim men hunted wild turkeys. They gathered clams and oysters, too.

There weren't any pumpkin pies at the first Thanksgiving. They did have cranberries, though.

The Indians showed the Pilgrims how to make popcorn.

It was winter when the Pilgrims landed. They did not have warm houses or enough food.

In the spring, Indians who lived nearby taught the Pilgrims how to grow corn and vegetables. At harvest, the Pilgrims planned a feast to thank God for their food. They invited their Indian friends.

Men hunted ducks and geese for the feast. Children gathered nuts and berries. Women made cornbread, fish stew, and other food. Indians brought deer meat. Everyone helped, and everyone celebrated together. Look at the graph. How many girls were there? How many boys?

This Pilgrim woman, along with seven other women, cooked for three days to feed 141 people!

The Pilgrims didn't have forks and spoons. They used seashell scoops.

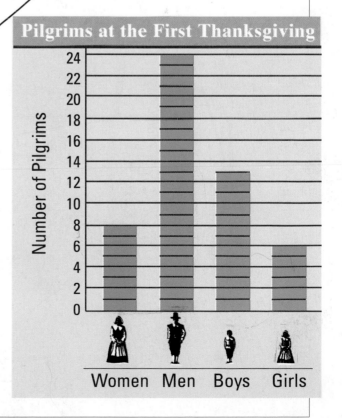

Pilgrims at the First Thanksgiving

Number of Pilgrims

Women Men Boys Girls

107

Fourth of July Night

The fireworks are a lot of fun.
I watch each giant spark
As it goes streaking up the sky—
Then lights up all the dark
In a lovely splashing splatter
Of a thousand silver stars,
In a tumbling, rumbling clatter
That goes echoing off to Mars.

Eleanor Dennis

Why do we celebrate the Fourth of July?

What are all the fireworks about? Why are there picnics and parades and flags? It's the Fourth of July, of course! Many Americans celebrate the Fourth of July. It's our country's birthday. Here is how this holiday started.

After the Pilgrims arrived, more and more people came to America. They lived in 13 different colonies. A **colony** is a group of people ruled by a country far away. The colonies were ruled by England, but the people wanted to rule themselves.

Leaders of the American colonies held a big meeting in the city of Philadelphia. There they wrote a special paper called the Declaration of Independence. It told England that the colonies wanted to be free. On July 4, 1776, the leaders of the colonies agreed to sign the paper. The Americans were willing to fight a war to win their freedom.

They won the war. Now every Fourth of July we say, "Happy Birthday, America!"

Why do we celebrate Presidents' Day?

Two of our most important presidents were born in February. They are George Washington and Abraham Lincoln. We honor them on Presidents' Day.

George Washington is sometimes called the father of our country. He is called this because he helped to win the war for our freedom from England. He was a strong and brave leader. After the war he became the first President of the United States.

Abraham Lincoln was President when the states in the North and the states in the South fought a terrible war.

A speech written by Abraham Lincoln ➤

Four score and seven years ago our fathers brought forth, upon this continent, a new nation, conceived in Liberty, and dedicated to the proposition that all men are created equal.

The North won the war, and the United States became one country again. On Presidents' Day, Abraham Lincoln is remembered for bringing our country back together.

Our country celebrates many other holidays. Use the timeline to find some of them.

Our Country's Holidays

Martin Luther King, Jr. Day   Memorial Day   Labor Day   Thanksgiving

Jan.	Feb.	March	April	May	June	July	Aug.	Sept.	Oct.	Nov.	Dec.

Presidents' Day   Fourth of July   Columbus Day

REVIEW

1. Why do people in our country celebrate holidays?
2. Why was Thanksgiving first celebrated?
3. What do we celebrate on the Fourth of July?
4. Why were George Washington and Abraham Lincoln important presidents?

Learning More

Holidays are fun. They are also interesting. We have a reason for celebrating each holiday. You know why we celebrate Thanksgiving. You can learn why we celebrate Columbus Day, too.

You can find out about Columbus Day or any other holiday in the library. A **library** is a place where you will find many books. Some books tell about a holiday, a person, or any other idea. The librarian can help you find books in the library.

What is the reason that we celebrate Columbus Day? We remember Christopher Columbus on this day. You can find out more about him in the library. The librarian will show you where to find books with information. Then you can learn more about Columbus.

Try It!

Pick a holiday that you want to know more about. Then go to the library and find a book that tells about this holiday. The librarian will help you. Find out why the holiday you pick is special.

Make a poster for the holiday. Show something on the poster that you learned in the library.

We Have One President

THINK

What does our President do?

Key Words

president
vote
ballot

What is the most important job you can think of? Many people think it is being President of the United States. The **President** is the leader of the American people. What do you think is the most important thing a President does?

The President tries to keep our country strong and to protect our freedom. The President tries to make sure that all of our laws are obeyed and that we are safe in our country.

Mt. Rushmore shows the faces of four presidents. ➤

Washington, D.C.

The White House

The President lives and works in the White House in the city of Washington, D.C. How do we choose our President?

Every four years, grown-up citizens in our country vote on who should be President. They **vote** by going to places such as schools in their neighborhoods. There they get a card or piece of paper called a **ballot.** They mark the ballot next to the name of the person they want for President. In some places, people use a voting machine instead of a ballot.

Being the President is an important job. Voting for the President is an important job, too!

REVIEW

1. What does our President do?
2. How do we decide who should be President?
3. What things would you do if you were President?

A Plan for Your School

In the United States, people choose the country's leader. They vote for the President.

You, too, can see what it is like to make a choice and to vote. Imagine that you can choose how your school will spend some money. The next page shows two plans for spending the money. You can choose one plan.

1. Read each plan.

2. Think about what is important to you and to your school.

3. Vote for one plan.

Plan 1

- Get more computers for school.
- Build a large computer classroom.

Plan 2

- Get more playground equipment.
- Make the playground bigger.

Now count the votes. Which plan got the most votes? The plan with the most votes wins.

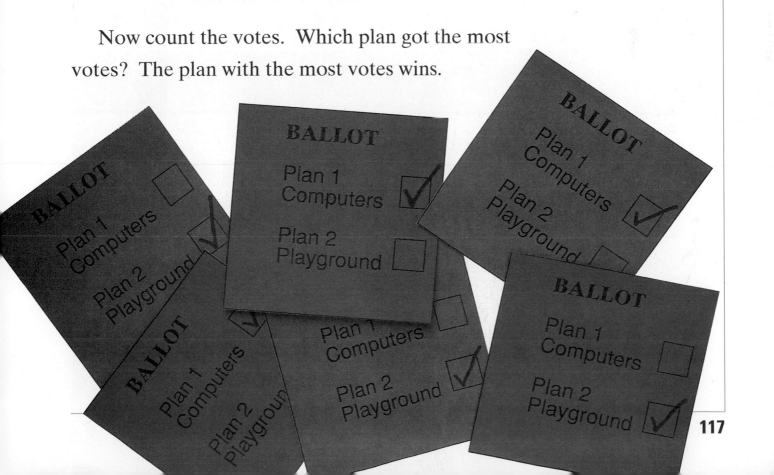

We Have Symbols

THINK

What do the flag and the Statue of Liberty stand for?

Key Word

symbol

Do you know why we have a flag? It would be very hard to draw a picture showing all the things our country stands for. Instead, we use symbols, such as our flag, to remind us of our country. A **symbol** is a picture or a thing that stands for something else. The flag stands for all the land and all the people and all the things we believe.

Look at the 50 stars on the flag. Each star stands for one of the 50 states in our country today. Each stripe stands for one of the first colonies. How many stripes are there?

Sometimes people try to show the flag in a special way. An artist made the flag below to show the different people who came to America. The names of some people who recently came to America are written in the stripes.

In busy New York Harbor stands another important symbol—the Statue of Liberty. She holds her torch high to tell the world that the United States is a free country. Here is what some second graders in St. Louis, Missouri, think about the Statue of Liberty.

"The Statue of Liberty means I can be whatever I want to be. I want to be a baseball player."
Christopher Bartley

Kieth Strong

"The Statue of Liberty looks like a lady. She has a torch in her hand and a book. She stands for freedom to all people."
Surayya Ibrahim

"The Statue of Liberty is big. I would like to go inside it. I want to go in her hat and look out."
Recardo Morris

Beth Ide won a prize for this quilt she made that shows the Statue of Liberty and the flag. Here is what she says.

"I think how important it is to have such a fine country. We can do anything we want as long as we are not hurting anyone else."

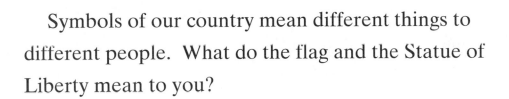

Symbols of our country mean different things to different people. What do the flag and the Statue of Liberty mean to you?

REVIEW

1. What do the flag and the Statue of Liberty stand for?
2. What do the stars and stripes on our flag stand for?
3. What other things do you think would be good symbols for our country?

The Statue of Liberty stands in New York Harbor and is a symbol of our free country. This story will tell you who built it and how it got to New York Harbor.

LITERATURE

THE STORY OF THE STATUE OF LIBERTY

Written by Betsy Maestro

Illustrated by Giulio Maestro

The Statue of Liberty stands on an island in New York Harbor. She is a beautiful sight to all who pass by her. Each year, millions of visitors ride the ferry out to the island. They climb to the top of the statue and enjoy the lovely view.

A young French sculptor named
Frédéric Auguste Bartholdi visited America
in 1871. When he saw Bedloe's Island in
New York Harbor, he knew it was just the
right place for a statue he wanted to build.

Bartholdi had created many other statues and monuments, but this one was to be very special. It was to be a present from the people of France to the people of America, as a remembrance of the old friendship between the two countries.

When Bartholdi got back to Paris, he made sketches and some small models. The statue would be a woman whom he would call Liberty. She would be a symbol of the freedom in the New World. She would hold a lamp in her raised hand to welcome people who came to America. She would be *Liberty Enlightening the World*.

The statue would be very large and very strong. Bartholdi wanted people to be able to climb up inside the statue and look out over the harbor from the crown and torch.

Many well-known artists, engineers, and craftsmen gave him ideas about how to build the statue. First, a huge skeleton was constructed from strong steel.

Many people worked together in a large workshop. Some worked on Liberty's head and crown. Others worked on her right hand which would hold the torch.

In her left hand she would hold a tablet with the date July 4, 1776, written on it. This is when the Declaration of Independence was signed.

The arm holding the torch was sent to Philadelphia for America's 100th birthday celebration in 1876. Afterward, it stood in Madison Square in New York City for a number of years.

Liberty's head was shown at the World's Fair in Paris during this time. Visitors were able to climb inside and look around. In this way, money was raised to pay for the statue.

Then, skin of gleaming copper was put onto the skeleton and held in place with iron straps. As the huge statue grew, all of Paris watched with great fascination.

Finally, in 1884, Liberty was completed. There was a big celebration in Paris. Many famous people came to see her. Only a few had the energy to climb all the way to the crown—168 steps!

Then began the hard work of taking Liberty apart for the long voyage across the Atlantic Ocean. Each piece was marked and packed into a crate. There were 214 crates in all. They were carried by train and then put on a ship to America.

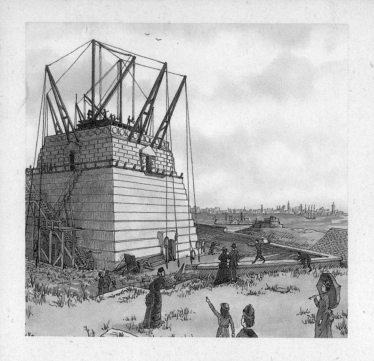

But in America people had lost interest in the Statue of Liberty. Money had run out and work on Bedloe's Island had stopped. The base for the statue was not finished. With the help of a large New York newspaper, the money was raised. People all over the country, including children, sent in whatever they could. By the time the ship reached New York in 1885, it was greeted with new excitement.

The work on the island went on and soon the pedestal was completed. Piece by piece, the skeleton was raised. Then the copper skin was riveted in place. Liberty was put back together like a giant puzzle. The statue had been built not once, but twice!

At last, in 1886, Liberty was standing where she belonged. A wonderful celebration was held. Boats and ships filled the harbor. Speeches were read, songs were sung. Bartholdi himself unveiled Liberty's face and she stood, gleaming in all her glory, for everyone to see. There was a great cheer from the crowd. Then President Grover Cleveland gave a speech.

Over the years, immigrants have arrived to begin new lives in America. To them, the Statue of Liberty is a symbol of all their hopes and dreams. She has welcomed millions of people arriving in New York by ship.

Every year on the Fourth of July, the United States of America celebrates its independence. Fireworks light up the sky above New York Harbor. The Statue of Liberty is a truly unforgettable sight—a symbol of all that is America.

What Do Citizens Do?

People who are born in a country are citizens of that country. Other people who move to a country can become citizens, too.

You have learned that citizens of our country are alike in some ways and different in some ways. But every citizen in our country has certain jobs, or duties.

A citizen should care for the land, animals, and plants in our country. A citizen should also care about the leaders and the symbols of our country.

All citizens must obey the laws.
Only grown-up citizens can vote.
   All of these things are part of
being a good citizen.

Unit 3 Review

Words

ballot
celebrate
citizen
colony
president
symbol
vote

Which of the two words best fits the sentence?

1. My mother is a **(symbol, citizen)** of this country.

2. Who will be the next **(ballot, president)** of the United States?

3. A **(symbol, colony)** is ruled by a country far away.

4. Each class member will **(celebrate, vote)** for class president.

5. Tony is marking his **(citizen, ballot)** with his choice for class president.

6. Monday we will **(vote, celebrate)** Lisa's birthday.

7. The eagle is a **(symbol, president)** that stands for our country.

Ideas

Think about what you have learned about our country. Look at the pictures on the next page. Write some sentences about each picture. Tell why these things help make us one country.

Skills

Go to the library. Ask your librarian to help you find a book about Abraham Lincoln or George Washington. Read about him. Write some sentences about what you have learned.

Activities

1. Work with your class to make a class flag. Use designs that stand for your class.
2. Abraham Lincoln often wore a special kind of hat called a stovepipe hat. Work with a partner to find some pictures of Lincoln wearing a stovepipe hat. Make hats like Abraham Lincoln wore.

Lincoln's Hat

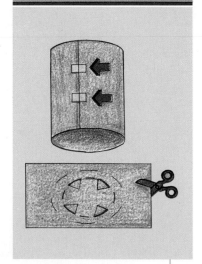

People Who Have Made a Difference

Tommy sits behind me
In Miss Abernathy's class.
When he grows up he wants to be
The man who mows the grass.

Lisa wants to write big books.
Andy wants to sing.
Paula says she'll sleep all day
And not do anything!

And as for me, I think I'll be
The captain of a ship.
I'll sail it to the moon and back—
Oh, what a lovely trip!

Making a Difference

Key Words

talent
interest

Our world is a big place, filled with many people. Each person can make a difference. You can, too!

How can you make a difference in such a big world? You may have a special talent. A **talent** is something you are good at, such as singing or playing a sport. Your talent can be shared with other people. Many people enjoy listening to a good singer or watching sports.

You may have special interests, too. An **interest** is something you like to do or to learn about, such as taking care of animals or learning about computers. How might a person's interest in taking care of animals make a difference in the world? That person may grow up to be an animal doctor and help animals—and their owners—feel better.

Often, the interests people have as children help them decide what to be when they grow up. Do you like to draw? Maybe you will grow up to be an artist. Look at the drawings in this book. An artist likc thc one shown here drew them. Maybe someday your pictures will be in books, too.

In this unit, you will read about people who have made a difference. You will learn what these people were like as children. You will learn how they used their talents and interests to make the world better.

REVIEW

1. How can one person make a difference in the world?
2. What are some kinds of talents and interests that people have?
3. What talents and interests do you have that could make a difference?

Alexa Canady

THINK

How does Alexa Canady help children?

Key Word

surgeon

"Could I ever be like Florence Nightingale?" thought Alexa Canady. Florence Nightingale was a famous nurse who helped sick soldiers long ago. When Alexa was a child, she read about this famous nurse. Alexa wanted to help others as Florence Nightingale did.

When Alexa Canady grew up, she became a surgeon. A **surgeon** is a doctor who does operations. Today Dr. Canady is a surgeon at Children's Hospital in Detroit, Michigan. One of the children she has helped is Justin.

After Justin was hurt playing soccer, he was taken to Dr. Canady. She asked him questions to help her figure out what was wrong. "Do you have headaches, Justin?" she asked. "Do things look blurry?"

Dr. Canady used special tools to help her find out what was wrong. She tapped Justin's knee with a rubber hammer. His foot should have jumped when she tapped his knee. It didn't, so something might be wrong.

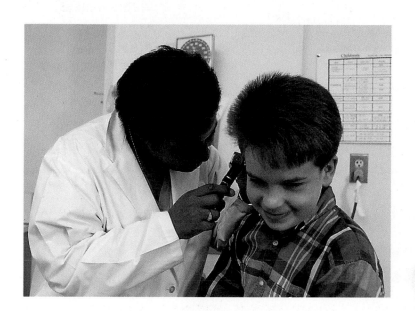

Next, Dr. Canady looked into Justin's ears with a special light. She asked Justin to walk in a straight line and to touch his nose. He could not do these things. "Tests will tell us more about what is wrong," Dr. Canady said. She decided to send Justin to a hospital for the tests.

When the tests were all over, Dr. Canady decided Justin needed an operation. Let's take a look at Dr. Canady as she gets ready for an operation.

A Surgeon

When: 7:00 A.M., Tuesday
Where: Children's Hospital
What: A surgeon gets ready
        for an operation.

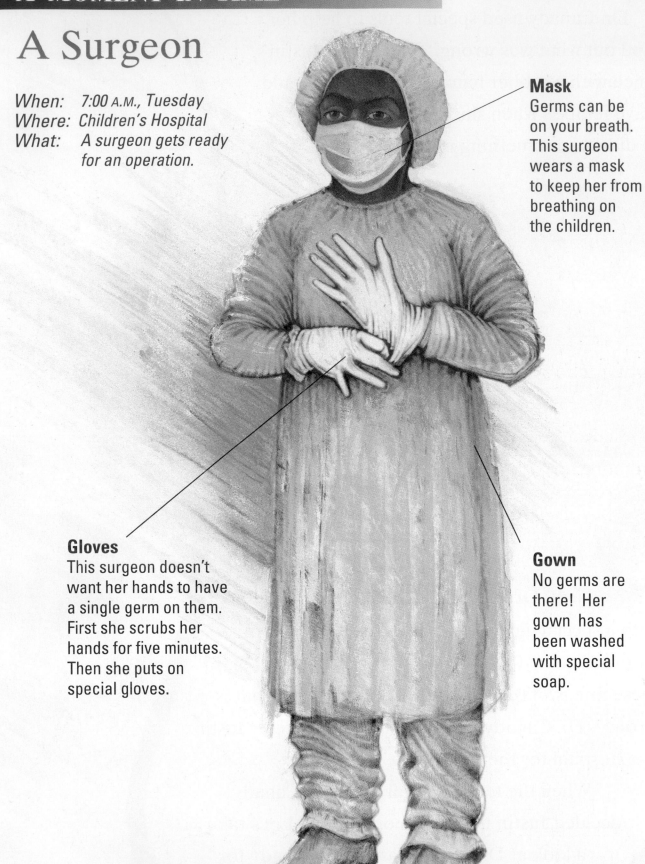

Mask
Germs can be on your breath. This surgeon wears a mask to keep her from breathing on the children.

Gloves
This surgeon doesn't want her hands to have a single germ on them. First she scrubs her hands for five minutes. Then she puts on special gloves.

Gown
No germs are there! Her gown has been washed with special soap.

Justin was worried before the operation, but Dr. Canady explained what would happen. After the operation was over, Justin stayed in the hospital for a while. Dr. Canady visited him every day to see how he was doing. Now Justin is back in school and playing with his friends.

Dr. Canady has helped many boys and girls like Justin. It took many years of study for her to become a surgeon. She is glad she studied so hard. Like Florence Nightingale, she can make people feel better.

REVIEW

1. How does Alexa Canady help children?
2. What tools does she use to find out what is wrong?
3. Who are the people who help you when you are sick?

Hope You Are Feeling Better!

How People Help

You have seen how Dr. Canady works to help people. Now find out how someone you know works to help people.

Get Ready

1. Choose an adult to talk to.
2. Write these questions.

What do you do in your job?
How do you help people?

Find Out

1. Talk to the person and ask the questions you wrote down.
2. Write or draw something to help you remember what the person tells you.

Move Ahead

1. Make a picture of how the person helps people.
2. Put your picture on a class poster.

Roberto Clemente

"Whack!" went the bat against the baseball. The crowd stood and cheered. Roberto Clemente had another hit! He was one of the best baseball players ever. He had more hits than almost anyone who ever played.

Roberto was born in Puerto Rico. He had always wanted to be an athlete. An **athlete** is someone who has a talent for sports. Roberto and his friends played baseball every day. They didn't have money to buy real baseballs. Instead, they wrapped old golf balls with string and tape.

The Clemente family was not rich, but the children were taught to share. Roberto never forgot this lesson.

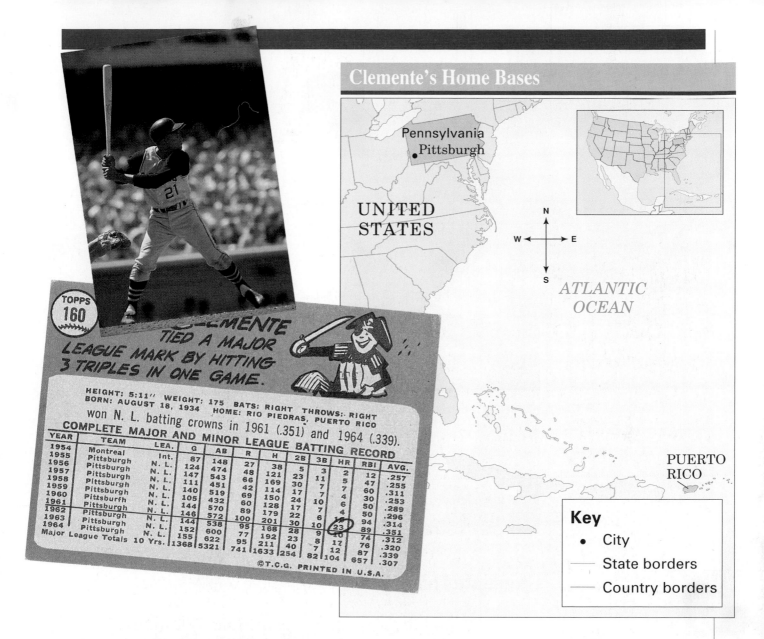

Clemente's Home Bases

Clemente Becomes Famous

As Roberto grew taller and stronger, he continued to practice baseball. He dreamed of playing on a major league team. The Pittsburgh Pirates asked him to play for them. Roberto lived in Puerto Rico, but he traveled to Pittsburgh every year to play baseball. Find Puerto Rico and Pittsburgh on the map.

Roberto Clemente became a great baseball player. Look at his batting record on the baseball card. How many home runs did he hit in 1961?

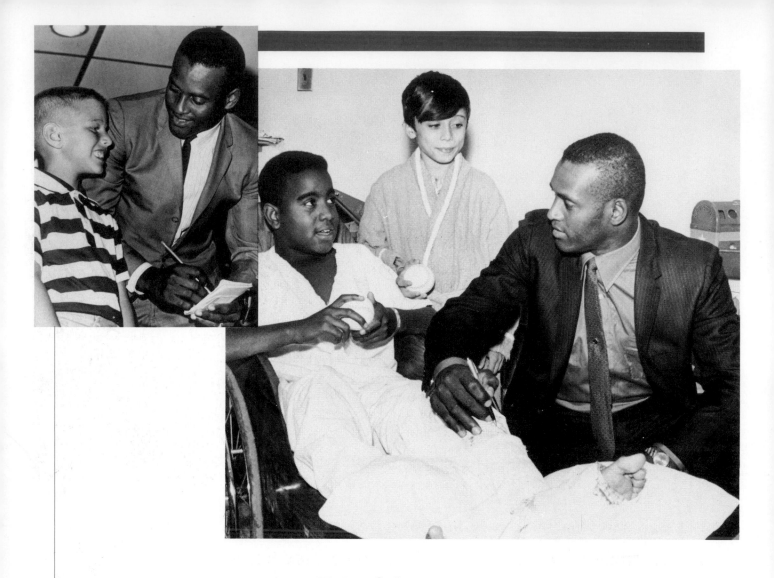

Clemente Helps Others

When he became a famous athlete, Clemente didn't forget about others. He often visited children in hospitals. He made sure families could get good care.

Roberto Clemente liked to teach young people about baseball. He wanted the children to be good athletes. He wanted them to care about each other, too.

In December of 1972, Roberto Clemente heard about an earthquake in another country. He wanted to help the people who were hurt.

Clemente Is Remembered

Even though it was the Christmas holiday, Clemente packed food, clothing, and medicine in boxes. He got on an airplane to help deliver the boxes.

Then a sad thing happened. The airplane crashed in the ocean. All of the people on it died. Clemente would never come home.

People cried when they heard about Clemente. They remembered him in many ways. He was chosen to be in the Baseball Hall of Fame. His picture was put on a special postage stamp.

Roberto Clemente is remembered because he was a great athlete. He is also remembered because he cared about others.

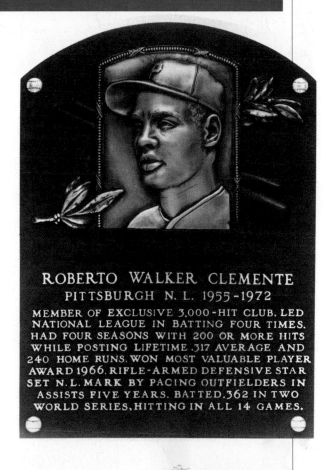

ROBERTO WALKER CLEMENTE
PITTSBURGH N. L. 1955-1972
MEMBER OF EXCLUSIVE 3,000-HIT CLUB. LED NATIONAL LEAGUE IN BATTING FOUR TIMES. HAD FOUR SEASONS WITH 200 OR MORE HITS WHILE POSTING LIFETIME .317 AVERAGE AND 240 HOME RUNS. WON MOST VALUABLE PLAYER AWARD 1966. RIFLE-ARMED DEFENSIVE STAR SET N.L. MARK BY PACING OUTFIELDERS IN ASSISTS FIVE YEARS. BATTED .362 IN TWO WORLD SERIES, HITTING IN ALL 14 GAMES.

Roberto Clemente
USA 20c

REVIEW

1. How did Roberto Clemente help others?
2. What are some ways people remember Roberto Clemente?
3. Why do we want to remember special people from the past?

What's the Big Idea?

The last lesson was about Roberto Clemente. You read about his childhood, how he became a baseball player, and how he helped others.

The story gave a lot of information about Roberto Clemente. What do you think the big idea of the lesson was? What was the most important thing you learned? It was that Roberto Clemente was a famous athlete who helped others. This is the **main idea** of the story. All the other sentences tell something about this main idea.

Every story has a main idea. The sentences in the story tell about this main idea.

Reread the story about Alexa Canady on pages 138–141. Decide what the most important idea is. Then pick the sentence below that tells the main idea.

1. Alexa Canady helped a boy named Justin.
2. Alexa Canady works in Detroit, Michigan.
3. Alexa Canady is a doctor who helps others.

All three of the sentences are true. Two sentences give small bits of information. One sentence tells what the story was mainly about. Which one is that? The third sentence tells the main idea in the story.

Try It!

Reread "The Banana Bunch" on pages 20–27. Think about what the story is mainly about. Then decide which of the following sentences tells the main idea of the story. Tell why you think this is the main idea and the other sentences are not.

1. Many people work to bring bananas to you.
2. Children like to eat bananas for lunch.
3. Food travels by ship.

Louis Braille

THINK

How did Louis Braille help other blind people?

Key Word

method

Imagine reading with your fingers! Could you read by feeling the letters? That is how Louis Braille learned to read.

Long, long ago, Louis Braille was a little boy who lived in France. When he was almost five years old, he became totally blind. But Louis's father still believed Louis could learn to read and write. He believed Louis would someday go to college. That would not be easy for Louis.

Since Louis could not see, he had to learn many things all over. He depended on his touch and on his hearing to tell him where he was and what was happening. It was hard for him to run and play.

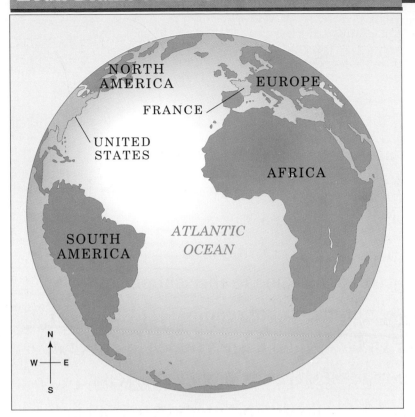

When Louis was seven years old, he went to school. Because he could not see pictures or words, listening was his only way to learn. He had to remember everything the teacher said.

Later, Louis went to a school that used a special method to teach blind children to read. A **method** is a way of doing or learning something. The students had to feel letters carved in wooden blocks. It took time to figure out each word by feeling the letters. Many students forgot the words by the time they got to the end of a line!

151

One day someone came to the school to show students a better method of reading. This method used paper with dots and dashes punched out of it. People read the messages by feeling the paper. Because people could use this method to read in the dark, it was called "night writing." This method was easier, and it gave Louis an idea.

Louis thought that raised dots would be easier to feel than holes in paper. When Louis was 15, he made a new method of reading, using six raised dots.

Braille Alphabet

A B C D E F G H I

J K L M N O P Q R

S T U V W X Y Z

It was a long time before the Braille method was used for teaching blind students. When Braille died, not many people knew of him or of his reading method.

Later, the school where Braille had been a student started using his method. Soon schools in the United States began to teach it, too. Today, there are machines and computers based on Braille's method. These machines help the blind read, write, draw, and play music. Louis Braille's method has helped blind people all over the world.

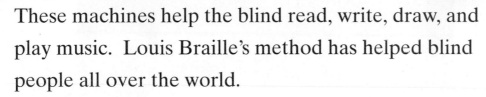

REVIEW

1. How did Louis Braille help other blind people?
2. Where did Braille get the idea for his method?
3. Look at the Braille alphabet on page 152. Write your name using Braille's alphabet.

Eleanor Roosevelt

THINK

How did Eleanor Roosevelt help others?

Key Word

human rights

"Look, here comes her plane!" All the people at the airport looked up. They were waiting to see Eleanor Roosevelt, one of the most famous women in the world. She had flown all the way across the Atlantic Ocean from America. She was coming to Switzerland for an important meeting with leaders from around the world. When the plane landed, many people were there to welcome her.

Speaking to a large crowd may be scary to many people. But it didn't seem as if anything in the world could frighten Eleanor Roosevelt!

It hadn't always been this way. When Eleanor was a little girl, she was scared of everything. She was afraid of animals, the dark, and thunderstorms. She was even afraid of other children. Most of all, Eleanor was afraid that no one would ever like her.

Eleanor Roosevelt was born over a hundred years ago. Her parents died before she was ten. Then she lived with her grandmother. She had few friends to play with, and she was sometimes unhappy and lonely. Slowly, she learned that she wanted to help others.

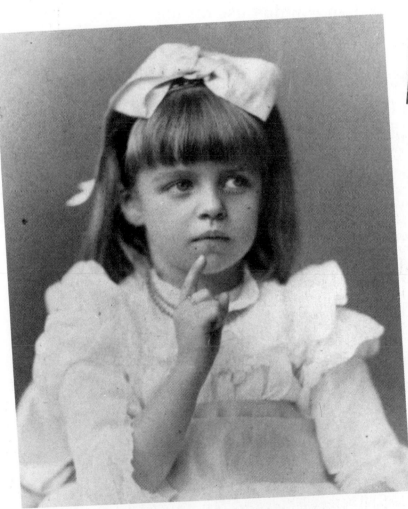

Eleanor Roosevelt Grows Up

When Eleanor Roosevelt grew up, she married Franklin Roosevelt. He became one of the leaders of our country. Franklin Roosevelt became sick and then couldn't use his legs. Mrs. Roosevelt knew her husband wanted to keep working even if he couldn't walk. So she traveled and made speeches for him.

When Franklin Roosevelt was elected governor of the state of New York, Mrs. Roosevelt visited schools and hospitals. She came home and told him how people needed help.

All of Eleanor Roosevelt's hard work wasn't just for her husband. She had her own projects. She started a furniture business to make new jobs for the poor. Then she helped run a girls' school. She also taught history and reading.

Later, Mrs. Roosevelt helped build homes for people in places where they could find new jobs.

Eleanor Roosevelt believed it did not matter if you were a man or a woman, white or black, young or old. All people were born free and equal and should be treated the same. She wanted everyone to have the same chance for a happy life. These things she believed in are called **human rights.**

When Franklin Roosevelt was elected President of the United States, Mrs. Roosevelt had more work than ever before. Now she had the whole country to visit!

Franklin Roosevelt was President for 12 years. When he died, Mrs. Roosevelt felt that her work was over. The rest of the world didn't agree! Everyone had learned to love her.

That same year, Eleanor Roosevelt flew to Switzerland for a meeting about human rights. There she helped write an important paper. The paper talked about how people in all countries should be treated equally.

Eleanor Roosevelt helped many people during her life. The shy little girl with no friends had grown up to be loved by people everywhere.

REVIEW

1. How did Eleanor Roosevelt help others?
2. What are some human rights?
3. What could you do to help others?

Thomas Edison

THINK

Who was Thomas Edison, and how did he change the world?

Key Words

invention
laboratory

"Where are you now, Tom?" Mrs. Edison called. She was worried. Young Thomas Edison often tried new things that got him into trouble. Once he set the barn on fire. Once he fell into a bin full of grain. *Now* where was he? Mrs. Edison found him in the barn getting up from a hen's nest. His pants were covered with egg. "Why were you sitting on those eggs?" Tom's mother cried.

"I wanted to see if I could hatch them," said Tom.

Even after he grew up, Thomas Edison kept trying to understand how things worked. He found new ways to make things work better. He built machines never thought of before. Each of these was an **invention** of his.

Edison sold some of his first inventions and used the money to start his own laboratory. His **laboratory** was a special building where he could work on his inventions.

Edison had ideas for many useful things. The light bulb was one of his ideas. He drew pictures to show how it might work. Many people worked with him to build this new invention.

He often worked all day and all night trying to get his light bulb to work right. When he got tired, he would just lie down and take a nap.

After trying for two years, Edison finally got the light bulb to work. The light bulb was to be one of his most important inventions.

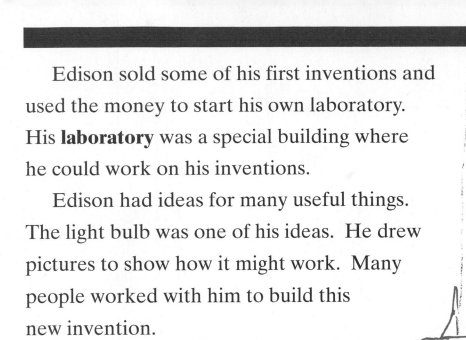

Edison and the Light Bulb

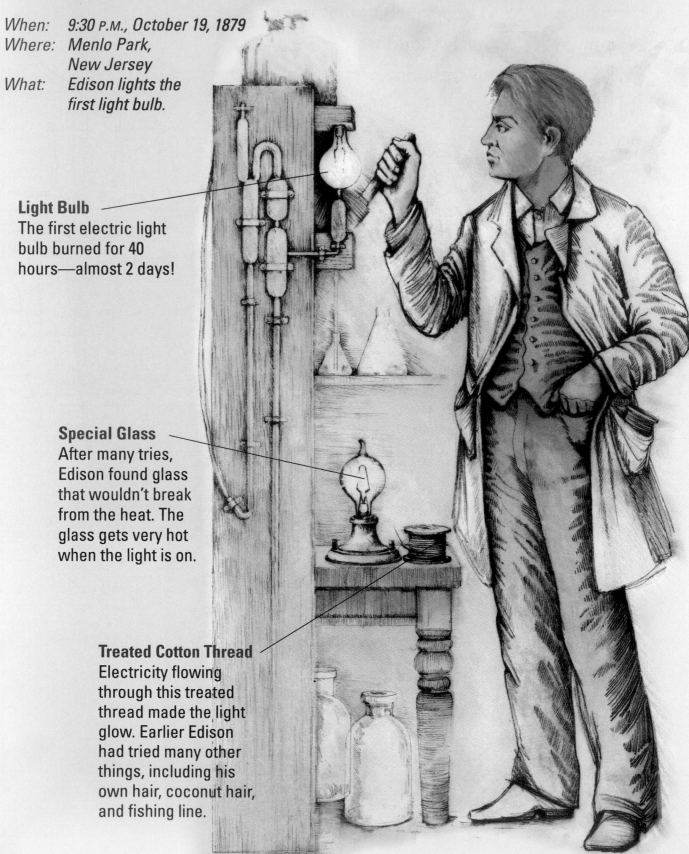

When: *9:30 P.M., October 19, 1879*
Where: *Menlo Park,*
New Jersey
What: *Edison lights the*
first light bulb.

Light Bulb
The first electric light
bulb burned for 40
hours—almost 2 days!

Special Glass
After many tries,
Edison found glass
that wouldn't break
from the heat. The
glass gets very hot
when the light is on.

Treated Cotton Thread
Electricity flowing
through this treated
thread made the light
glow. Earlier Edison
had tried many other
things, including his
own hair, coconut hair,
and fishing line.

Thomas Edison was one of the world's greatest inventors. His ideas have changed the lives of people everywhere. The chart below shows some of his inventions that you still use today.

Some of Edison's Inventions

THEN		NOW
	Edison invented the phonograph, a machine that played sound. What machines do you use that can play recorded sound?	
	Edison invented the projector, a machine that showed moving pictures. How do today's movie projectors look different?	
	Edison invented the electric light bulb. How many uses for the electric light bulb can you think of?	

REVIEW

1. Who was Thomas Edison, and how did he change the world?
2. Where did Edison work on his inventions?
3. How do you think Edison's invention of the light bulb changed the world?

Who Thought of It First?

You have learned about the things Thomas Edison invented. Almost everything you use was invented by someone! A simple idea can sometimes lead to an invention.

Toothbrush

William Addis put holes in a small bone. Then he pulled pieces of brush through the holes and glued them. People had been cleaning their teeth with rags. They really liked these new toothbrushes!

Zipper

Whitcomb Judson got tired of spending 15 minutes every morning putting on his shoes. That's how long it took to button up the high-button shoes people wore long ago. So Judson invented the zipper! The first zippers were used just for shoes. Today, zippers are used to close everything from sweaters to sleeping bags.

Sandwich

John Montagu, the Fourth Earl of Sandwich, liked to play games so much that he would not stop to eat. One day he put some meat between two pieces of bread. Then he could hold his food in one hand and keep playing games!

Basketball

James Naismith wanted a fun and safe indoor sport. He used a soccer ball and two peach baskets. It was so much fun that people started playing basketball outdoors, too!

An invention is a new thing or a new way of doing something. Inventions change our lives in small ways and in big ways. What would you like to invent someday?

Yoshiko Uchida

THINK

How does Yoshiko Uchida help us understand others?

Key Words

author
custom

Do you have a friendly neighbor you could tell a story about? Yoshiko Uchida had lots of them when she was your age. Now she is an **author.** She writes books about people from her past. Read about Mr. Wada and Emi from her book *The Birthday Visitor*.

Emi swung open the squeaky gate to their backyard and found old Mr. Wada sitting in a canvas chair, wearing his eyeshade and taking a little nap. His wrinkled face looked half green beneath the celluloid shade.

"Hello, Ojii-chan," Emi called in a loud voice. He liked being called Grandpa, since he didn't have any grandchildren of his own.

Mr. Wada bestirred himself and smiled at Emi.

"Ah, come to see us at last, have you?" he shouted, as though she were just as deaf as he.

Emi went to his good ear and shouted back, "I was here last Friday."

But Mr. Wada didn't pay attention to what she said. "Well now, would you like to see my old friend in the pond?" he asked cheerfully. And without waiting for an answer, he got up creakily and stirred the murky water of his fish pond. In a moment, the enormous speckled carp nosed his way to the surface, nipping the old man's finger as though it were a delicious worm.

"Hello there, old friend," Mr. Wada greeted him warmly. "How do you feel today? Look who's come to see us."

"Wouldn't you rather have a pet dog, Ojii-chan?" Emi asked as she watched. A dog would at least wag his tail and lick his hand, she thought.

But the old man shook his head. "What could be nicer than a pet carp?" he asked. "He doesn't bark, he doesn't dig up the moss in my garden, and he doesn't have to be walked. He just lives peacefully at the bottom of his pond and lets me be. When I want to see him, I just stir up the water and there he is."

Yoshiko Uchida,
from *The Birthday Visitor*

Growing Up

Yoshiko Uchida grew up in Berkeley, California. She lived in a small house with her parents and her sister. Yoshiko's parents were both from Japan. Many of their neighbors in Berkeley were also from Japan. Yoshiko had many Japanese friends—people like Mr. Wada in *The Birthday Visitor*.

Yoshiko's family lived in California, but they followed many Japanese customs. A **custom** is a group's special way of doing something. A custom Yoshiko liked was Dolls' Day. On that day Yoshiko's mother set Japanese dolls on a table. The dolls were not to be played with, just looked at. What beautiful dolls they were!

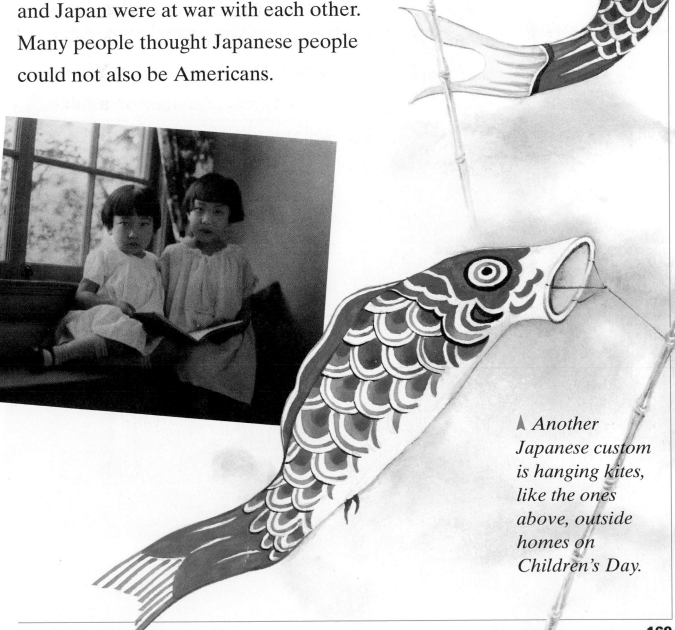

Yoshiko loved Japanese poems and stories, too. She loved the Japanese American people in her neighborhood. But she was an American, and she loved her family's new country, too.

Yoshiko Uchida wanted to be both Japanese *and* American. Sometimes this was hard. During those years, America and Japan were at war with each other. Many people thought Japanese people could not also be Americans.

▲ *Another Japanese custom is hanging kites, like the ones above, outside homes on Children's Day.*

169

Uchida's family and other Japanese Americans had to leave their homes and go to prison camps built by the Army. While Uchida was there, she taught second grade. When the war was over, the camp was closed and everyone left to make new homes.

Becoming an Author

Uchida continued to teach, but she decided to become an author. She wanted to write about the Japanese American neighbors she had when she was small. She wanted to tell people about Japanese customs. She wanted people to understand and love the people she loved.

Uchida has written many stories about her own life—like the story about Emi and Mr. Wada. When Uchida visited Japan, she learned many old Japanese tales. She has retold these tales in her books. She has also written books about people she met there.

Now people read her books and learn what it was like to be a little Japanese American girl in Berkeley, California. They learn about the customs of Japanese Americans. They read Uchida's stories and imagine what it is like to be a boy or girl in Japan.

REVIEW

1. How does Yoshiko Uchida help us understand others?
2. What was one Japanese custom Yoshiko Uchida liked when she was a child?
3. Write a story and draw pictures about a grandparent or a neighbor.

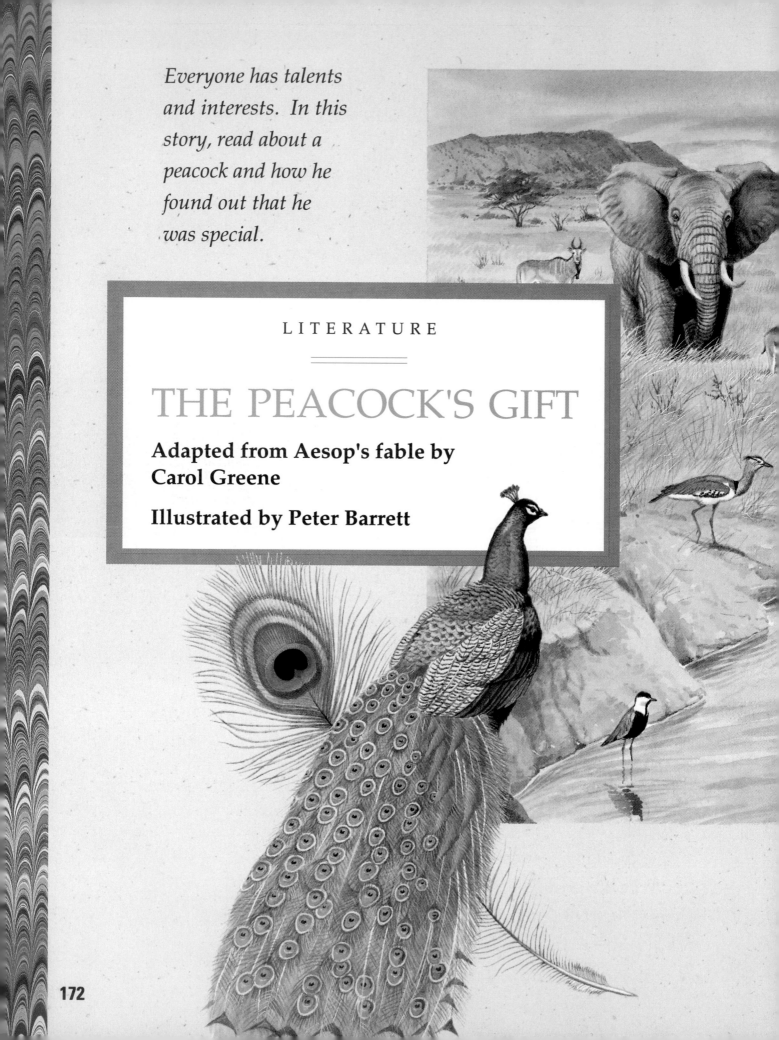

*Everyone has talents
and interests. In this
story, read about a
peacock and how he
found out that he
was special.*

THE PEACOCK'S GIFT

**Adapted from Aesop's fable by
Carol Greene**

Illustrated by Peter Barrett

172

Lion and Lioness ruled the animal
world and they ruled it very well.
One day they sent for the birds
to see if each was doing its job.

"My job is to fly," said Eagle. "My strong wings carry me high into the blue sky. Then I look down on the green earth and see that all is well in the world."

"My job is to sing," said Nightingale. "Each night my song puts the world to sleep and sends it sweet dreams."

"My job is to speak," said Parrot. "I can speak as people do and make the world laugh. Yoo hoo! Shut the door! I want a cracker!"

"And what about you?" Lion and Lioness asked Peacock. "What is your job?"

Peacock's head dropped and so did his tail. "I have no job," he said. "I can barely fly at all. My song is ugly. And I cannot speak as people do. I am useless."

"What?" cried Eagle. "Why, your beauty makes me feel strong. When I look at you, I see blue sky and green earth. Then I want to fly."

"Your beauty makes me feel glad," said Nightingale. "When I look at you, I see rainbows and waterfalls. Then I want to sing."

"Pretty bird! Pretty bird!" said Parrot. "You are a pretty bird, Peacock."

"So that is your job,
Peacock," said Lion and Lioness.
"Each has a gift to share. Eagle
has strength. Nightingale has
song. Parrot has speech. You
have beauty."

"Imagine that!" said Peacock.
He lifted his head and spread
his beautiful tail.

Unit 4 Review

Words

Which of the two words best fits the sentence?

1. The phonograph is an important **(surgeon, invention).**

2. Which **(custom, athlete)** will win the race?

3. Kate is the **(author, method)** of many books.

4. Meg's **(athlete, interest)** is learning about bugs.

5. A **(custom, surgeon)** washes carefully before an operation.

6. Louis Braille invented a new **(method, athlete)** of reading for blind people.

7. Jeremy is working on his invention in the **(human rights, laboratory).**

8. A **(talent, custom)** is a group's special way of doing something.

9. Johnny has a lot of **(invention, talent)** for drawing.

10. Eleanor Roosevelt believed in **(human rights, custom)** for people everywhere.

athlete
author
custom
human rights
interest
invention
laboratory
method
surgeon
talent

Ideas

Think about the people in the pictures below. Write a sentence about each person. Tell how each person made a difference in the world.

Skills

Reread "The Peacock's Gift" on pages 172–176. Decide what is the most important idea in the story. Then pick the sentence below that tells the main idea.

1. The lion is the king of the animals.
2. Each bird makes the world better in its own special way.
3. Peacocks have beautiful feathers.

Activities

1. Bring something to class that shows a talent or an interest you have. Tell your class about it.
2. Work with one or two other students. Together, act out something from one of the stories in this unit. Have the rest of the class guess whose life you are showing.

Information Bank

THE WORLD

ARCTIC OCEAN

**NORTH
AMERICA**

UNITED STATES

PACIFIC
OCEAN

ATLANTIC
OCEAN

Equator

**SOUTH
AMERICA**

PACIFIC
OCEAN

— Country borders

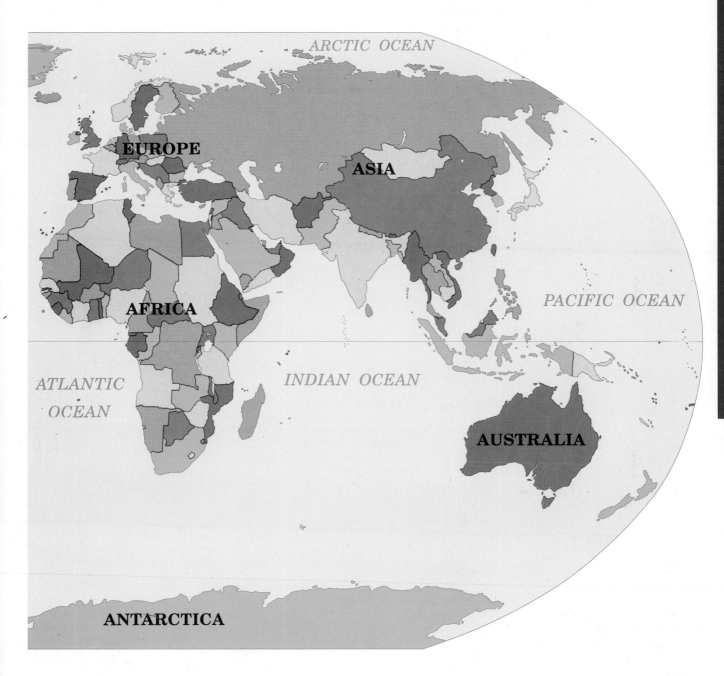

ARCTIC OCEAN

EUROPE

ASIA

PACIFIC OCEAN

AFRICA

INDIAN OCEAN

ATLANTIC
OCEAN

AUSTRALIA

ANTARCTICA

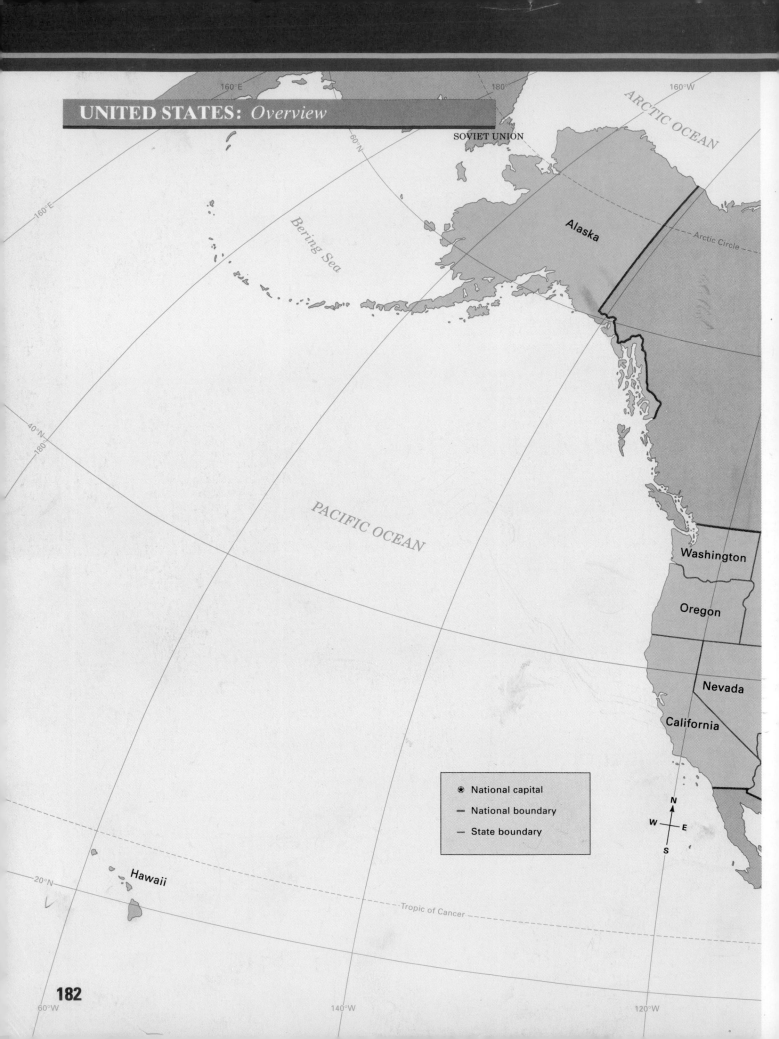

ARCTIC OCEAN

SOVIET UNION

Alaska

Arctic Circle

Bering Sea

PACIFIC OCEAN

Washington

Oregon

Nevada

California

⊛ National capital

— National boundary

— State boundary

N
W · E
S

Hawaii

Tropic of Cancer

140°W 120°W 100°W 80°W 60°W 40°W 20°W

GREENLAND

Hudson Bay

CANADA

60°N

40°W

60°N

L. Superior

Montana

North Dakota

Minnesota

Michigan

Maine

Vermont

New Hampshire

L. Huron

Idaho

South Dakota

Wisconsin

Ontario

New York

Massachusetts

Rhode Island

40°N

Wyoming

Iowa

L. Michigan

L. Erie

Connecticut

Nebraska

Illinois

Indiana

Ohio

Pennsylvania

New Jersey

60°W

Utah

Colorado

Washington

Delaware

Maryland

Kansas

Missouri

West Virginia

Virginia

Kentucky

Arizona

New Mexico

Oklahoma

Arkansas

Tennessee

North Carolina

ATLANTIC OCEAN

South Carolina

Mississippi

Georgia

Texas

Alabama

Louisiana

Florida

0 250 500 mi.

0 250 500 km

Azimuthal Equal-Area Projection

BAHAMAS

MEXICO

Gulf of Mexico

CUBA

20°N

PUERTO RICO (U.S.)

100°W 80°W

THE UNITED STATES

ALASKA

ARCTIC OCEAN

Alaska

CANADA

PACIFIC OCEAN

PACIFIC

OCEAN

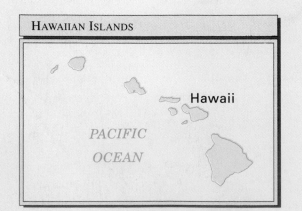

HAWAIIAN ISLANDS

Hawaii

PACIFIC

OCEAN

Washington

Oregon

Idaho

Montana

Wyoming

Nevada

California

Utah

Colorado

Arizona

New Mexico

MEXICO

N
W — E
S

CANADA

Lake Superior

North Dakota

Minnesota

Michigan

Lake Huron

Maine

Vermont

New Hampshire

South Dakota

Wisconsin

Lake Michigan

Lake Ontario

Massachusetts

Rhode Island

Connecticut

New York

Nebraska

Iowa

Lake Erie

Pennsylvania

New Jersey

Illinois

Indiana

Ohio

Delaware

Maryland

Kansas

Missouri

West Virginia

Virginia

Kentucky

North Carolina

Oklahoma

Arkansas

Tennessee

South Carolina

ATLANTIC

Texas

Mississippi

Alabama

Georgia

OCEAN

Louisiana

Florida

Gulf of Mexico

185

mountain
a raised part of the land,
much higher than a hill

lake
a body of water with
land all around it

hill
a raised part of the land,
smaller than a mountain

forest
a large area of
land where many
trees grow

valley
low land between
hills or mountains

river
a large stream of water that
runs into a lake, ocean, or
another river

harbor
a safe area of water near
land where ships can stop

shore
the land along the edge
of a lake, sea, or ocean

island
a body of land with
water all around it

ocean or **sea**
a salty body of water
that covers a large area
of the earth

ancestors   Members of your family, starting with your parents, who were born before you.   Page 44

citizen   A member of a country.   Page 104

country   A land with its own laws, symbols, and people. Page 16

athlete   A person who is trained in sports.   Page 144

colony   A community of people ruled by a country far away.   Page 109

crops   The plants farmers grow to sell or use.   Page 9

author   A person who writes books.   Page 166

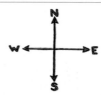

compass rose   A symbol showing the directions of north, south, east, and west. Page 6

custom   The special way a group of people does something.   Page 168

ballot   The paper on which people mark their votes. Page 115

consumer   A person who buys things.   Page 38

depend   To need someone. Page 3

celebrate   To honor or remember a special day, event, or person.   Page 106

continent   A large area of land with water around it. Page 15

diagram   A drawing that shows and names the important parts of something. Page 34

east The direction in which the sun rises. If you face north, east is on your right. Page 6

history All things that have happened in the past. Page 58

laboratory A place in which to work on inventions. Page 161

education Going to school to learn facts, skills, and ideas. Page 88

holiday A day to celebrate someone or something special. Page 50

library A place with many books you can borrow. Page 112

factory A place where machines are used to make things. Page 11

human rights The belief that all people are equal and should be treated fairly. Page 158

main idea The most important point, or idea, of a story. Page 148

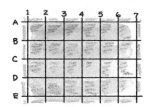

grid A set of lines that divide an area on a map into small squares. Page 70

interest Something you like to do or to learn about. Page 136

map key A list of the symbols being used on a map. Page 5

harvest Picking or gathering crops when they are ripe. Page 10

invention A new machine or way of doing something. Page 160

method A way of doing or learning something. Page 151

north The direction of the North Pole. On most maps, north is at the top. Page 6

south The direction of the South Pole. On most maps, south is at the bottom. Page 6

tradition Something that is done a certain way for many years. Page 59

ocean A large body of salt water. Page 15

suburb A community near a big city. Page 64

vote To help make a decision by having your choice counted. Page 115

President The leader of the United States and of the American people. Page 114

surgeon A doctor who does operations. Page 138

weather What the air is like—hot or cold, wet or dry. Page 20

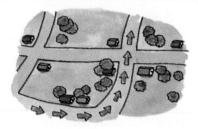

route A path or road of travel. Page 25

symbol A picture or a thing that stands for something else. Page 118

weave To lace threads together to make cloth. Page 92

seaport A city by the sea with a harbor used by ships. Page 23

talent Something a person is naturally good at. Page 136

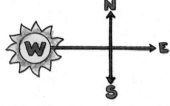

west The direction in which the sun sets. If you face north, west is on your left. Page 6

ACKNOWLEDGMENTS

Text *(continued from page iv)*

28–33 (xv) from pp. 13–22 from *Truck Song* by Diane Siebert. Illustrated by Byron Barton. (Crowell) Text Copyright © 1984 by Diane Siebert. Illustrations Copyright © 1984 by Byron Barton. Reprinted by permission of Harper & Row, Publishers, Inc. **45** "Everybody Says" by Dorothy Aldis reprinted by permission of G. P. Putnam's Sons from *Everything and Anything* by Dorothy Aldis, copyright 1925–1927, copyright renewed 1953–1955 by Dorothy Aldis. **72–81** *Watch the Stars Come Out* by Riki Levinson, illustrated by Diane Goode. Text copyright © 1985 by Riki Friedberg Levinson. Illustrations copyright © 1985 by Diane Goode. Reprinted by permission of the publisher, Dutton Children's Books, a division of Penguin Books USA Inc. **108** "Fourth of July Night" by Eleanor Dennis from *Poetry Place Anthology,* copyright © 1983 by Scholastic, Inc. Reprinted by permission of Scholastic, Inc. **122–29** *The Story of the Statue of Liberty* by Betty Maestro, ill. by Giulio Maestro. Text: Copyright © 1986 by Betty Maestro. Ill: Copyright © 1986 by Giulio Maestro. By permission of Lothrop, Lee & Shepard (A Division of William Morrow & Co.) **153** From *Amelia Bedelia Helps Out* by Peggy Parish. Text: Copyright © 1971 by Margaret Parish. By permission of Greenwillow Books (A Division of William Morrow & Co.). Braille transcription, 1986 by Phyllis Hultz. *Seedlings,* Braille Books for Children, 8447 Marygrove Drive, Detroit, Michigan, 48221. **166–67** (text) *The Birthday Visitor* by Yoshiko Uchida. Text Copyright © 1975 by Yoshiko Uchida. Text reprinted by permission of Yoshiko Uchida. (illustrations) Reprinted with permission of Charles Scribner's Sons, an imprint of Macmillan Publishing Company from illustrations by Charles Robinson in *The Birthday Visitor*. Illustrations copyright © 1975 Charles Robinson.

Special Thanks: Begaye family; Dr. Alexa Canady; Manwell family; Sanchez family; Schweizer family; Suos family; Wambles family; Winslow family.

Illustrations

Literature border design by Peggy Skycraft.

Ligature 5, 6, 7, 12, 41, 131, 133, 142. **Peter Barrett** 172–173, 174, 175, 176. **Brian Battles** 150, 178. **Howard Berelson** 140, 160, 162. **Charlie Bernatowicz** 45, 113(b), 143. **Carolyn Croll** 106–107, 111, 133(t). **Jim Dickinson** 18. **Susan Dodge** 117. **Roger Dondis** 47, 66, 89. **Len Epstein** 2–3, 38, 39. **Ruth Flanigan** 9, 71, 99. **Simon Galkan** 163. **Jackie Geyer** 17, 23–24(b). **Robert Levine** 82. **Ben Mahan** 67. **Dan McGowan** 186. **Rebecca Merrilees** 34, 35. **Larry Nolte** 187, 188, 189. **Jan Palmer** 36–37. **Judy Pelikan** 44. **Michael Pessalato** 107(r). **Kieth Strong** 120. **Mou-sein Tseng** 169. **Kyuzo Tsugami** 57, 58, 59, 61, 94, 95. **Fred Winkowski** 20, 21, 22(t), 23(t), 24, 25, 26, 27, 149. **Other: 113(t)** Illustration from *Columbus* by Ingri & Edgar Parin D'Aulaire, copyright © 1955 by Doubleday, a division of Bantam, Doubleday, Dell Publishing Group, Inc. Used by permission of the publisher. **113(c)** Illustration reprinted with permission of Charles Scribner's Sons, an imprint of Macmillan Publishing Company from *The Columbus Story* by Alice Dalgliesh, illustrated by Leo Politi. Copyright 1955 Alice Dalgliesh and Leo Politi; copyright renewed © 1983.

Maps

R. R. Donnelley & Sons Company Cartographic Services 102–3, 180–81, 182–83, 184–85. **JAK Graphics** 14–15, 16, 24, 49, 57, 65, 85, 91, 145, 151.

Photographs

SK—Stephen Kennedy; TIB—The Image Bank

Front cover Peter Bosey. **Back cover** David Hiser, Photographers/Aspen. **xvi–1** © Frank Oberle, Photographic Resources. **2–3** SK. **4** © Grant Heilman, Grant Heilman Photography. **7** Rick Benkof. **8** © Mike Clemmer (tr,bl); SK (cl,br). **9** SK. **10** SK (tl); © Mike Clemmer (tr,cl,b). **11** Mike Phillips (tr,bl); SK (cl,br). **12** SK. **13** Rick Benkof (tl); SK (r). **14** SK. **17** © Stephen Wilkes, TIB. **18** SK. **19** SK. **21** © George Ancona. **22** © George Ancona, International Stock Photo. **23** Mississippi State Port Authority. **25** © Chris Jones, The Stock Market (l); © Mike Jaeggi (cr). **26** © Mike Jaeggi. **27** SK. **35** © Bullaty/Lomeo, TIB. **38** SK. **39** SK. **42–43** © Walter Hodges, Allstock. **44** SK. **45** Diane Penson Archive. **46** Patrick Tehan (tl); SK (cr,tl); © C. Schmeiser, Unicorn Stock Photos (bl); © Joe Viesti (br). **48** © Melanie Freeman (tr, bl); © Steve Dunwell, TIB (cr). **49** © In Stock, Photo Researchers, Inc. (t); © John Spragens, Jr., Photo Researchers, Inc. (b). **50** SK (t); © Eileen Blumenthal (bl); © Peter Arnold (br). **51** Suos family (t); SK (b). **52** SK, Eric P. Newman Numismatic Education Society. **53** Suos family; SK (r). **54** © Steve Dunwell, TIB (t); © Wally McNamee, Woodfin Camp & Associates (cl); Bob Daemmrich, The Image Works (bl); Eileen Blumenthal (br). **55** © Robert Harbison (t); © Tom Pix, Peter Arnold (b); SK (br). **56** © Michael Garland, Onyx. **57** © Kal Muller, Woodfin Camp & Associates. **59** © Michael Garland, Onyx (tr); SK (cl,cr). **60** © Ken Ross, Joe Viesti Associates (tl); SK (cl,br); © Larry Kolvoord, Joe Viesti Associates (cr). **61** © Michael Garland, Onyx. **62** © Mary Ann Brockman (l); SK (tr,b). **63** © Robert E. Daemmrich, TSW—Click/Chicago Ltd. (tl); © D. & J. Heaton, Uniphoto Picture Agency (b); SK (r). **64** Scott Raffe. **65** Schweizer family. **66** SK (l); Schweizer family (r). **67** SK, Missouri School for the Blind (t); SK. **68** Mike Phillips (tl); © Robert Barclay, Grant Heilman Photography (tr); Schweizer family (b). **69** Schweizer family. **70** Scott Raffe. **83** SK. **84** Cathy Lander-Goldberg. **85** SK. **86** from *The Old West: The Pioneers,* Harald Sund, © 1974 Time-Life Books Inc. (tl); © Guhl, Photographic Resources (tr); Mississippi Department of Economic Development (cr); © Frank Oberle, Photographic Resources (b). **87** SK (tr,b); St. Louis Mercantile Library (cl). **88** Cathy Lander-Goldberg (tr); Winslow family (bl); SK (br). **89** Cathy Lander-Goldberg. **90–91** Monty Roessel. **92** Monty Roessel (tl,bl); © Frank Oberle, Photographic Resources (cl). **93** SK; Hubbell Trading Post (tl). **94** © Monty Roessel (t); Cathy Lander-Goldberg (b). **95** Monty Roessel. **96** SK (t); Rick Benkof (b). **97** Rick Benkof. **99** © Roy Roper, Gamma-Liason (l); © Robert Colton, Black Star (r). **100–101** © E. C. Stengler, Allstock. **104** © Michael Pettypool, Uniphoto Picture Agency (t); © Eunice Harris, Photo Researchers, Inc. (b). **105** © Gene Staver, Gas Company (tl,cr); © Peter Miller, Photo Researchers, Inc. (tr). **106–7** SK. **108** © Al Sapperwhite, TIB. **108–9** SK. **109** Culver Pictures (tl); © Gene Staver, Gas Company (br). **110** Library of Congress (t,b); Gilbert Stuart, Historical Pictures Services (l). **111** Matthew Brady, 1864, Laurie Platt Winfrey, Inc.; **112** © Joe Viesti Associates; **113** SK. **114** © UPI/Bettman Newsphoto (t); © D. Dietrich, FPG International (b). **115** © Don Sparks, TIB (tl); © Paul Conklin, Uniphoto Picture Agency (tr); SK (cr). **116** SK. **117** SK. **118** © Raphael Macia, Photo Researchers, Inc.; **119** © Costa Manos, Magnum Photos Inc. (tl); © Pete Saloutos, Photographic Resources (tr); © Anthony Russell, Pentagram (b). **120** © Peter Miller, TIB. **120–21** SK. **121** Robin Brown (tl); © Michael Quakenbush, TIB (tr). **130** Rick Benkof. **131** Rick Benkof (t); © Bob Daemmrich, The Image Works (b). **133** © Wally McNamee, Woodfin Camp & Associates (tc); © Robert Kristofik, TIB (r); © Louis Goldman, Photo Researchers, Inc. (bl); The White House (bc). **134–35** © Debra Lex. **136** © Benn Mitchell, TIB (cl); SK (bl); © Brent Jones (br). **137** © Cathlyn Melloan, TSW—Click/Chicago Ltd. (tl); SK (tr,cr). **138** Jerome Madig. **139** Jerome Madig (l); SK (r). **141** Jerome Madig (t); SK (b). **142** SK. **143** SK. **144** SK, The Sporting News (c); SK, © Topps (r). **145** © Focus on Sports (t); SK, © Topps (b). **146** © UPI/Bettman Newsphotos (l); Pittsburgh Pirates (r). **147** National Baseball Library (t); SK, U.S. Postal Service (b). **148** © Jerry Wachter, Focus on Sports (l); Pittsburgh Pirates (r). **149** Jerome Madig. **151** SK, Terry Wilson. **152** SK. **153** SK. **154** FDR Library. **155** FDR Library (l); UPI/Bettman Newsphoto (r). **156** Historical Pictures Service, Inc. (tl,br); FDR Library (tr); FDR Library, C.P. Newell, 1915 (bl). **157** FDR Library (t); UPI/Bettman Newsphoto (b). **158** SK (t); FDR Library (bl); UPI/Bettman Newsphoto (br). **159** UPI/Bettman Newsphoto (t); FDR Library (b). **160** Culver Pictures (cl); Edison Laboratory National Monument, NJ (bl). **161** Edison Laboratory National Monument, NJ (tr,bl); The Granger Collection, NY (cr). **164** The Granger Collection, NY (t); © Mary Root, Root Resources (r); SK (bl); © Talon, Inc. (br). **165** Historical Pictures Service, Inc. (t); Naismith Memorial Basketball Hall of Fame (bl,br); **168** Gary Miyataki, Kari Kanesaka. **169** © Yoshiko Uchida. **170** © Yoshiko Uchida. **171** SK (t); Deborah Storms, © Yoshiko Uchida (b). **178** l to r: © Focus on Sports; Deborah Storms, © Yoshiko Uchida; © Jerome Madig; © Edison Laboratory National Monument, NJ; © Historical Pictures Service, Inc.

Picture research assistance by Carousel Research, Inc. and Meyers Photo-Art.